Senior Centers
in
America

Recent Titles in
Contributions to the Study of Aging

Geriatric Medicine in the United States and Great Britain
David K. Carboni

Innovative Aging Programs Abroad: Implications for the United States
Charlotte Nusberg, with Mary Jo Gibson and Sheila Peace

The Extreme Aged in America: A Portrait of an Expanding Population
Ira Rosenwaike, with the assistance of Barbara Logue

Old Age in a Bureaucratic Society: The Elderly, the Experts, and the State in
American History
David Van Tassel and Peter N. Stearns, editors

The Aged in Rural America
John A. Krout

Public Policy Opinion and the Elderly, 1952–1978
John E. Tropman

The Mirror of Time: Images of Aging and Dying
Joan M. Boyle and James E. Morriss

North American Elders: United States and Canadian Perspectives
Eloise Rathbone-McCuan and Betty Havens, editors

Hispanic Elderly in Transition: Theory, Research, Policy and Practice
Steven R. Applewhite, editor

Religion, Health, and Aging: A Review and Theoretical Integration
Harold George Koenig, Mona Smiley, and Jo Ann Ploch Gonzales

Philanthropy and Gerontology: The Role of American Foundations
Ann H. L. Sontz

Perceptions of Aging in Literature: A Cross-Cultural Study
Prisca von Dorotka Bagnell and Patricia Spencer Soper, editors

Residential Care for the Elderly: Critical Issues in Public Policy
Sharon A. Baggett

Senior Centers in America

JOHN A. KROUT

CONTRIBUTIONS TO THE STUDY OF AGING, NUMBER 14

Erdman B. Palmore, *Series Adviser*

GREENWOOD PRESS
New York • Westport, Connecticut • London

Library of Congress Cataloging-in-Publication Data

Krout, John A.
  Senior centers in America / John A. Krout.
    p. cm.—(Contributions to the study of aging, ISSN
  0732–085X ; no. 14)
  Includes index.
  Bibliography: p.
  ISBN 0–313–26058–3 (lib. bdg. : alk. paper)
    1. Day care centers for the aged—United States. 2. Aged—
  Services for—United States. I. Title. II. Series.
  HV1461.K76 1989
  362.6'3—dc20   89–11993

British Library Cataloguing in Publication Data is available.

Library of Congress Catalog Card Number: 89–11993
ISBN: 0–313–26058–3
ISSN: 0732–085X

First published in 1989

Greenwood Press, Inc.
88 Post Road West, Westport, Connecticut 06881

Printed in the United States of America

The paper used in this book complies with the
Permanent Paper Standard issued by the National
Information Standards Organization (Z39.48–1984).

10 9 8 7 6 5 4 3 2 1

Copyright Acknowledgments

The author and publisher gratefully acknowledge permission to use the following:

Ralston, Penny, "Senior Center Research: Policy from Knowledge?" in *Critical Issues in Aging Policy: Linking Research and Values,* edited by E. Borgatta and R. Montgomery. Copyright © 1987 by Sage Publications, Inc. Reprinted by permission of Sage Publications, Inc.

Leanse, Joyce, and Sara B. Wagner, *Senior Centers: Report of Senior Group Programs in America* (1975): 29, National Council on the Aging, Inc.

Krout, John A., "Senior Center Activities and Services: Findings from a National Survey," *Research on Aging* 7(3): 455-71. Copyright © 1985 by Sage Publications, Inc. Reprinted by permission of Sage Publications, Inc.

Krout, John A., "Knowledge of Senior Center Activities among the Elderly," *Journal of Applied Gerontology* 3(1): 71-81. Copyright © 1984 by Sage Publications, Inc. Reprinted by permission of Sage Publications, Inc.

Krout, John A., "Senior Center Linkages with Community Organizations, *Research on Aging* 10(2): 258-74. Copyright © 1988 by Sage Publications, Inc. Reprinted by permission of Sage Publications, Inc.

Senior Center Standards: Guidelines for Practice (1978): 5, National Council on the Aging, Inc.

Cohen, Morris, "The Multipurpose Senior Center" in *Senior Centers: A Focal Point for Delivery of Services to Older People* (1972): 1-17, National Council on the Aging, Inc.

Wagener, Lin, and Patricia Carter, *Building Community Partnerships* (1982): 39, National Council on the Aging, Inc.

IN MEMORY OF
MY GRANDPARENTS

Sara Raffensperger Krout
Palled Bertram Krout
Emily Kruegl Swinehart
Lester Emett Swinehart

AND MY BROTHER-IN-LAW

Thomas Hadyn Nobbs

Contents

Preface

This book has been written in the belief that senior centers are an important feature of the community-based support system of the elderly that has generally been neglected and sometimes misunderstood by gerontological researchers. Thus, it attempts to describe, integrate, analyze, and draw conclusions from the research that is available and bring into focus the research questions that should be addressed in the future. The approach is eclectic and holistic in that many different facets of senior centers and their use are woven together to answer the questions what are senior centers, what do they do, how do they do it, what impact do they have, and what roles do they play in the lives of the elderly and in the aging services network.

But this is not intended to be a book by a researcher for researchers only. The basic questions and issues explored in the pages that follow should be of interest and concern to practitioners and policy planners and makers. The information on senior centers needed to make policy and planning decisions simply does not exist. Some senior center issues, such as user versus nonuser characteristics, have received a fair amount of attention. Most other topics have barely been touched. This is a somewhat curious state of affairs given the large number of senior centers and senior center users in this country and their visibility both locally and nationally.

This book is limited to the study of senior centers in the United States, not because they or something like them are not found in other countries, but because international comparisons seem somewhat premature given the rather meager level of research and data available in this country. The intended audience includes upper-level students, researchers (academic or otherwise), aging network practitioners including (but not limited to) senior center directors, policy planners and makers, and persons of any age interested in senior centers or aging services.

Finally, it is most likely that the research or writings of some students of senior centers have been inadvertently excluded from this book. Such omissions are unintentional and I apologize to those who feel their contributions on this topic may have been overlooked. In addition, I regret any misinterpretations or inaccuracies in my presentation of the work of others. These too have been unintentional. It is my sincere hope that those who read this book will gain a greater insight into senior center issues and a heightened sense of the need to explore these issues much more fully in the future.

Acknowledgments

This book represents the culmination of almost a decade of research and reflection on senior center issues. Thus, a large number of individuals have helped me better understand this topic through formal and informal exchanges of ideas over the years. While all of these people deserve acknowledgment for their encouragement and insight, I would like to give special thanks to the following: Carol Beddingfield, Mike Cooley, Jean Coyle, Ken Ferraro, Penny Ralston, Betty Ransom, and Lin Wagener.

I would like to express a special appreciation to the American Association of Retired Persons Andrus Foundation for its generous support of my senior center research. This book would not have been written without the research opportunities afforded by this support. I am also grateful to the staff of Greenwood Press who worked to see this project completed in a professional and timely manner. Special thanks go to Marlene Chizmadia of SUNY-Fredonia's Office of Sponsored Programs, Research Services and Economic Development for her efforts in typing (or should I say word-processing) this book. I continue to marvel at her skill, speed, and most of all, patience with projects such as this.

As always, my spouse, Bobbi, has adjusted to the demands book-writing inevitably places on one's home life with support, understanding, encouragement, and good cheer. Thank you one and all.

List of Tables

1

Introduction

The purpose of this book is to collect, integrate, and analyze existing information on senior centers in order to increase awareness among researchers, practitioners, and policy makers of what these organizations are and what they do. Since it identifies research gaps and needs, this book is also a call to gerontologists to focus their analytical skills more closely on senior centers. But it is also intended to assist practitioners and policy makers by bringing issues of concern into better focus. However, this is not a book on the planning or operation of senior centers. The major focus is on contemporary senior centers: what they are like as organizations, the activities and services they provide, the characteristics of center participants, the role(s) senior centers play in the lives of the elderly and in the aging services network, the changes they have undergone over time, and the major policy issues involving senior centers now and in the future. To understand fully these issues, senior center developments and activities must be viewed within the context of national aging policy and funding decisions as well as the changing demographic makeup of the nation's elderly. It must be explicitly recognized that senior centers and their users are characterized by a rich and complex diversity that deserves and requires great caution in regard to sweeping conclusions and statements of truth.

No one theory or particular framework is used in this work. In fact, the relatively sparse literature available on senior centers, especially in regard to theories or models, suggests there is much to be done before researchers begin to test elaborate explanations of senior center operation or use. This book can best be described as holistic and eclectic; it incorporates the writings and research of academics and others from a variety of disciplinary backgrounds.

Table 1.1
Definitions of Senior Centers

Author	Definition
Maxwell, J. (1962)	A program of services offered in a designated physical facility in which older people meet at least two days or more each week under the guidance of paid leaders performing professional tasks. The senior center may be a single purpose or multipurpose agency established as a result of community planning based on the unmet needs of older people in a given community. The basic purpose of such centers is to provide older people with socially enriching experiences which would help preserve their dignity as human beings and enhance their feelings of self-worth.
Frankel, G. (1966)	A senior center is a physical facilty open to senior citizens at least five days a week and four hours a day, year-round, and operated by a public agency or a nonprofit organization with community planning which provides under the direction of paid professional leadership three or more of the services for senior citizens listed below: 1. Recreation 2. Adult education 3. Health 4. Counseling and other social services 5. Information and referral services 6. Community and voluntary services
Older Americans Act Title V, Section 501(c), (1973)	The term 'multipurpose senior center,' means a community facility for the organization and provision of a broad spectrum of services (including provision of health, social and educational services and provision of facilities for recreational activities) for older persons.
Leanse, J. & Wagener, L. (1975)	A program directed to older adults, meeting at least once weekly on a regularly scheduled basis and providing some form of educational, recreation or social activity.
National Institute of Senior Centers (1978)	A senior center is a community focal point on aging where older persons as individuals or groups come together for services and activities which enhance their dignity, support their independence, and encourage their involvement in and with the community.

Table 1.1 (continued)

Author	Definition
	As part of a comprehensive community strategy to meet the needs of older persons, senior center programs take place within and emanate from a facility. These programs consist of a variety of services and activities in such areas as education, creative arts, recreation, advocacy, leadership development, employment, health, nutrition, social work and other supportive services.
	The center also serves as a community resource for information on aging, for training professional and lay leadership and for developing new approaches to aging programs.

Source: P. Ralston. (1987, 203–204). Senior center research: Policy from knowledge? In E. Borgatta and R. Montgomery (Eds.). Critical issues in aging policy: Linking research and values. Newbury Park, CA: Sage. Reprinted by permission of Sage Publications, Inc.

WHAT IS A SENIOR CENTER?

Before proceeding any further, it is necessary to devote some attention to an important definitional issue. What is a senior center? At first brush this may seem to be a trivial or mundane question. After all, almost everybody knows what a senior citizens' center is. However, attention to this question provides a good introduction into some of the issues covered throughout this book and lays a common ground for readers and author alike. It is also important to recognize that the various definitions applied to the term senior center over the years have had and continue to have important implications for how these organizations are viewed in regards to aging policy issues.

There have been, as one might expect, a number of definitions given to the term senior center. Table 1.1 presents five definitions that have appeared over a twenty-five year period. A reading of these definitions reveals that there is little agreement as to how many days or hours of operation or what number or mix of programs are required for senior center status. Some commonalities do emerge, however. Four of the five definitions indicate that a senior center is a physical facility, that it results from or is part of a community planning process, and that it offers a wide variety of services and activities. Three of the definitions explicitly note a regular schedule of activities, while only two refer to a paid professional staff and a purpose. In addition, the definition found in the Older Americans Act amendments of 1973 adds the word "multipurpose" to the term senior center, while the National Institute of Senior Centers (NISC) definition of 1978 characterizes senior centers as "community focal points." Each definition notes that such places and the programs they offer are for older persons, without reference to any particular age. This is somewhat problematic, for the chronological age used to classify people as old has important implications. Most Americans think of the elderly as those aged sixty-five and over, because of Social Security and because most of the data presented on the elderly refer to that age. But, individuals need only be aged sixty or over to qualify for programs funded by the Older Americans Act, and senior centers sometimes drop their "membership" age down to fifty-five and allow people of any age to join if their spouse meets the requirements.

These observations, then, suggest the following working definition: Senior centers are designated places that play important roles in the aging services network to make a broad spectrum of activities and services available to older persons on a frequent and regular basis as a part or result of a community planning process. Although there is some logic to leaving the term "older" undefined, it is used here to refer to individuals aged sixty and over. This definition would exclude senior groups (often called clubs) that meet infrequently or for only one or two activities. Thus, many church-related senior groups and other senior clubs that meet once a week or less, and usually for purely social purposes, do not qualify as senior centers under this definition. This exclusion should not be taken as a criticism of these groups or a denial of the important role they play in the lives of many older Americans.

Such a working definition is quite broad and reflects what senior centers generally should do. This breadth is necessary because changes in the elderly population, and in public and private sector programs, have interacted with countless community-level variations to produce an ever-changing mosaic. As shall be seen, senior centers come in all shapes and sizes. It might be agreed that to be a true senior center, an organization has to offer a specific set of health, social, educational, and recreational experiences. Yet these functions can occur to different degrees in different ways, and with vastly different resources, in the various centers across the country.

This working definition does not adopt the term "multipurpose" as used in the Older Americans Act's definition. While this term has its appeal, it is also quite vague: does it mean multipurpose with regard to types of individuals served, content of programming, or nature of goals? The use of this word most likely reflects particular historical or political influences, or was simply a buzzword of the time. Most senior centers, as defined here, are multipurpose. Similarly, NISC's 1978 identification of senior centers as "community focal points" for the elderly is not adopted here. As will be discussed in detail later on in the book, the great appeal of the label "focal point" is surpassed by its even greater ambiguity. While senior centers may or may not act as focal points, it seems arguable to make such a function a requirement of senior center designation.

Having said this, it appears that one very important ingredient is lacking in this working definition. Maxwell (1962, 7) touches on this element when he notes that centers provide "socially enriching experiences" that "help preserve their dignity as human beings and enhance their feelings of self-worth." Senior centers provide many users with an opportunity for meaningful interaction with other people of similar background, interests, and perhaps most importantly, life experiences. For some, the senior center is the focal point of their daily interaction with others, and it provides many of their primary group relationships.

A significant percentage of their friends and perhaps their closest confidant may also have been gained through attendance at a senior center. Indeed, The National Council on the Aging (Leanse and Wagener, 1975) reports that 84 percent of the center participants interviewed as part of a national study indicated having a confidant, and that half of these confidants were also center members. Senior center activities and other senior center participants can be primary elements of how some elderly define themselves and the world around them. Of course, the centrality of the senior center as a vehicle for "connectedness" and a provider of a sense of belonging and self-definition varies from user to user and center to center. Some elderly may attend a center for a daily or weekly event and focus their lives on noncenter interactions and relationships. For others, the senior center provides primary group relationships that are not available elsewhere.

Thus, it seems appropriate to add several ideas to the working definition presented earlier. One is that senior centers provide opportunities for meaningful social interaction with others. A second is that such social interaction often encompasses deep and enduring friendships; a third is that center participation can foster a sense of belonging to the group and community and contributes to positive feelings of self-worth. The working definition of senior center now becomes:

designated places that play important roles in the aging services network, making a broad spectrum of activities and services available to older persons on a frequent and regular basis as a part or result of a community planning process. They provide seniors with opportunities for social interaction that can encompass strong friendships and contribute to positive feelings of self-worth and community belonging.

This is meant to be a working definition that points out the essential elements of senior centers. The degree and ways in which senior centers exhibit these elements varies considerably in reality. In many ways, the chapters that follow simply examine these various elements to gain a fuller understanding of what they mean.

THEORIES AND MODELS

It should be pointed out that very little attention has been given to building theories or models of senior centers (Krout, 1983a; Ralston, 1987). Ralston (1987) notes that three types of models have received some attention by researchers. These include models based on physical facilities (Jordan, 1978); programs (Leanse and Wagener, 1975; Maxwell, 1962; Ralston, 1983); and senior center participants (Taietz, 1976). Each of these will be discussed briefly.

Jordan (1978), an architect by training, develops a four-fold typology of senior centers based on physical facilities. In his schema, center facilities are classified as donated, shared, renovated, or new. Maxwell (1962) differentiates between centers based on programs—either single service or multiservice. This program model has been expanded by Leanse and Wagener (1975) and Ralston (1983). Leanse and Wagener (1975) categorize centers based on their size and complexity and made four designations: multipurpose senior center, senior center, senior club, and programs with special activities for the elderly.

Ralston (1983) categorizes senior centers based on the nature of their current programming: senior clubs, congregate meal or nutrition sites, and multipurpose senior centers. She finds that data on number and types of activities and services, staffing and scheduling patterns, and funding sources are important factors in differentiating between these three levels. Another author (Fowler, 1974) has suggested three different criteria by which to categorize senior centers: activities generated (services, activities, individual services and casework, or a combination); administrative type—centralized (one facility), decentralized (several locations), combined (centralized location with satellites), or multiple (operations with some level of connection); and origin of services (center staff only, center staff and other agencies, etc.). Cohen (1972) differentiates senior centers from clubs. Senior centers have the following characteristics: community visibility based on a good facility and easy identification; central location for services; an ability to serve as a focal point and as a bridge to the community; and a program purpose that focuses on the individual, family, and community.

Taietz (1976), on the other hand, bases his model on the characteristics of senior center users. He has found that senior center participants are more involved in the community and organizations than nonparticipants, and concluded that senior centers functioned more as voluntary organizations than as social agencies. While Taietz's model has received considerable attention from gerontologists, it is based on a study that does have limitations: the data were collected from senior center users in upstate New York only. The conclusion that a voluntary organization as opposed to a social agency model best describes senior centers may well be true for those centers. But other senior centers, even in the early 1970s, might well have been characterized differently, and fifteen years of federal, state, and local initiatives have changed many older senior centers and spawned a new generation of these organizations. Indeed, it would appear that senior centers often have attributes that would be accurately described by both models.

The work of Taietz, Fowler, and others has been important. These researchers have attempted to identify factors salient to the nature of senior centers, the form and function of centers, and the types of experiences they provide their users. But these ideas have not been built upon or tested by other students of senior centers in any systematic way. And these attempts have been severely limited largely because they are based on studies of a small number of senior centers at one point in time. The diversity and changes experienced by centers have not been captured well.

THE IMPORTANCE OF SENIOR CENTERS

A book-length manuscript on senior centers would appear to be a significant and worthwhile endeavor for at least seven reasons. First, by virtue of numbers alone, senior centers should be receiving considerably more attention from scholars. After all, by the late 1970s an estimated 5,000 centers were operating in this country (U.S. Senate, 1979), a number that has since at least doubled (Schulder, 1985). The current National Council on the Aging senior center and club mailing list has over 17,000 entries. The sometimes fuzzy boundaries between senior centers and clubs, and the fluid nature of senior groups themselves, make it difficult to state with precision how many senior centers really do exist. Yet 10,000 or more social organizations, all bound by a common orientation to providing supportive experiences to the elderly, would certainly appear to merit closer examination by the gerontological community.

Second, there have been any number of local level examinations of senior centers by various agencies for rather narrow purposes of program assessment, planning, and funding. And a number of studies have been conducted by university-based gerontologists. But with the exception of *Little House* (Schramm and Storey, 1962), a book length study of one senior center in California, no book-length manuscripts exist on this topic. In most basic terms, a book on senior centers is needed to assemble in one place what can be said about these organizations based on available studies and to challenge other scholars to dispute, revise, and build on its findings and conclusions.

Third, it is fairly well-recognized by professionals and lay people alike that senior centers have come to play an important role in the lives of a significant number of elderly Americans. Senior centers generally have high degrees of visibility in local communities and most elderly know where senior centers in their area are located. The National Center for Health Statistics (NCHS) reports (1986) that data from its 1984 national Supplement on Aging reveal that 15 percent of the aged sixty-five and over attended a senior center in the previous year and 8 percent received hot meals there. These percentages translate into four and two million elderly individuals. An undetermined number of sixty-to sixty-five-year-olds should be added to those figures. Others (Pothier, 1985) put the total number as closer to ten million. Once more, the number of senior center attenders is from four to twelve times greater than that reported for any other community service for the elderly. A national survey conducted ten years earlier (Harris & Associates, 1975) reported that 18 percent of the elderly nationwide had attended a senior center or club in the past year.

Fourth, national legislation (especially the Older Americans Act and its amendments) has repeatedly focused on the importance of senior centers. Hundreds of millions of dollars have been allocated at the federal level and have passed through states and localities to establish and operate senior centers. Centers receive substantial amounts of state and local funding as well. Area Agencies on Aging frequently designate senior centers as "focal points" to assist in the planning, coordination, and delivery of comprehensive services to the community dwelling elderly. Senior centers must be considered to understand the operation and consequences of federal, state, and local aging policy and programs.

Fifth, in some ways the growth of senior centers comprises a social movement. The rapid growth in number and activities of senior centers in the 1970s was accompanied by the birth of organizations that, both locally and nationally, have acted as advocates not only for their own particular interests, but for the interests of the elderly in general. At the national level, the most visible of such organizations is the National Institute of Senior Centers (NISC) of the National Council on the Aging (NCOA). Thus, senior centers are part of the "politics of aging," locally and nationally.

Sixth, senior centers provide, either directly or through referral, a large number of services to a significant number of older persons. Traditionally, these persons have been the "young-old," who are relatively healthy and socially active. Supporting such a group could be viewed as preventive social support. However, as the elderly in society age, senior centers will increasingly be faced with a user population that is more frail and in need of more health-related supportive services. The ability of senior centers to adjust to this dynamic will be of considerable importance not only to senior center users, but also to policy makers and planners ever watchful for ways to support frail elders in the community and to reduce the spectrum of long-term care costs.

Finally, a better understanding of what senior centers do, how it is done, and who they do and do not serve in America today is vital to a consideration of the senior center of tomorrow. What can, or should, the senior center in the year 2000 look like? What changes can or should take place in programming, funding, organizational structure, participant targeting and so on? The increasing number of elderly, especially those seventy-five and over, and the "aging in place" of center participants since the 1970s, create a demographic imperative for the examination of all institutions and organizations significantly touched by the elderly. This imperative is intensified by broader social and economic realities such as the federal deficit, the struggles of communities to foster economic and social development, and the changing nature of health care. A fully informed consideration of the role senior centers will take in the aging network of the future requires a better understanding of their role today.

POINTS OF DEPARTURE

It is useful at the outset of a book for an author to identify major themes or points that will be developed throughout the course of his or her work. Sometimes these themes reveal assumptions (or biases) the author holds in regard to the topic at hand, and sometimes they form a thesis or argument the author wishes to examine. This book does not present a single thesis. Rather, it attempts a holistic examination of senior centers. The discussion that follows identifies a number of themes that act as points of departure for such a holistic study. They have grown out of almost a decade of research on senior centers by the author. These themes also serve as a set of assumptions to be developed and critically examined as this narrative unfolds.

The first is that senior centers provide a wide range of important and positive experiences for their users. The benefits exist in areas such as health, recreation, education, social contact, and self-image, to name but a few. Research by the author (Krout 1982, 1988) has shown that senior center participants overwhelmingly perceive their center experiences as positive and beneficial. However, it should be noted that very little empirical evidence has been collected on the specific outcomes or impacts of senior centers for the elderly participants and on the aging services network in general. Nor is it posited here that senior centers are appropriate for all older individuals. One focus of this book will then be to examine senior centers' importance for and impact on the elderly.

A second major theme is that senior centers play important, sometimes pivotal, roles in the support systems of the elderly. Senior centers often serve as an important source of informal support for the elderly by providing opportunities for the initiation and maintenance of friendships both in and outside center activities. These may develop into close relationships and continue even after an individual ceases center participation. In addition, the role of the senior center in the formal support system of the elderly is also significant. It is essential to view senior centers as a spoke in the often complex wheel of proprietary, not-for-profit, and public agencies that provide activities and services to the elderly. Thus, it is important to include a consideration of the characteristics of senior centers and the relationships they have with other organizations. The author's research on senior center "linkages" and "focal point" status (Krout, 1986, 1987, 1988) has attempted to examine these interorganizational functions, and will be reviewed in this book. A second focus will be on the role that senior centers play in the community in general and formal service network in particular.

Related to this second theme is the need to place senior center patterns and change within the history of federal aging policy. Senior centers, like hospitals, oil companies, or schools, can only be fully understood with reference to actions taken by institutions and individuals with power. While the impacts of these actions may not be understood or even noticed by senior center users, they have had enormous impact or what senior centers do, who they do it to, and how they do it. By the same token, senior centers are themselves holders of some power, and they play a role in shaping the allocation of resources. A third focus will then be on this dynamic and changing interplay between senior centers and larger policy actors and issues.

A fourth theme is that senior centers must also be viewed as an outgrowth of local conditions and needs. While social scientists typically strive to draw generalizations about social phenomena like senior centers, one must be reminded that their function and form vary considerably. This variation is not random, but can be understood as a consequence of the social and historical forces at the local level. These local variations and other factors have produced a rich diversity of senior center organizations. The often contradictory findings reported by researchers may well attest to the considerable diversity of centers in terms of organizational structure and resources, activities and services offered, and characteristics of elderly participants. It is oversimplistic, for example, to speak of an "average" senior center or center user, just as it is inaccurate to portray the elderly as a homogeneous group. Elderly individuals, even those who attend the same center, participate in senior centers for many different reasons and evidence widely divergent patterns of participation. Thus, another focus of this book is on senior center diversity and variation.

Finally, a fifth major theme is that senior centers, both in theory and practice, must be examined critically for both strengths and weaknesses. Many senior center practitioners themselves would agree with the statement that senior centers are not for everyone. The majority of elderly do not attend senior centers and ancedotal accounts from across the country suggest that senior centers are currently having some difficulty in attracting the "young-old." This trend brings attention to the question of the appropriateness of senior center programming. In addition, some gerontological observers (Daum and Dobrof, 1983; Guttmann and Miller, 1972; Matthews, 1979) have found fault with both the image of old age that is suggested by senior centers and the quality and effectiveness of their programming. Other issues that need to be addressed include the degree to which senior centers service the more frail or at risk elderly, and the degree to which senior centers should rely on public funding. Thus, the final theme is that senior centers have limitations requiring examination.

SOURCES OF INFORMATION

As is the case with most books, extensive use is made of the writings of other researchers. In addition, the work of more practitioner oriented literature such as that produced by the National Institute of Senior Centers of the National Council on Aging is also included. Some data from the 1984 Supplement of the National Center for Health Statistics Survey (NCHS, 1986) are cited. This supplement includes data from a nationally representative sample of almost 19,000 individuals aged sixty and over living in the community.

Finally, data from the author's own studies of senior centers will be used extensively as well. These studies have focused on both senior center participants and participation patterns and on senior centers as organizations. One of these projects focused on the service knowledge and utilization patterns of the elderly living in a small city (Krout, 1983a, 1983b). Particular attention was paid to the knowledge and use of the local senior center. A second project involved a survey of 755 senior centers in thirty-one states and collected descriptive data on the organization, staffing and programming of these centers (Krout, 1983c).

In 1986–87, the author studied the linkages senior centers maintain with other community organizations in providing services to the elderly for a national sample of 235 centers (Krout, 1987). The most recent research project examined participation in eight senior centers in Western New York. This study investigated reasons for the variation in and the impact of senior center participation, and also explored reasons for the cessation of center participation and the characteristics of ex-center users (Krout, 1988). All of these research projects have been funded by the American Association of Retired Persons (AARP) Andrus Foundation. It is hoped that the use of these varied types and sources of information will lead to a more accurate and balanced portrayal of senior centers in America.

ORGANIZATION OF BOOK

This book attempts to provide a comprehensive and critical consideration of the information currently available on senior centers in America. This information is organized into nine chapters including a final chapter devoted to an overall summary and concluding remarks. The first eight chapters cover the following topics: introduction to the book; history of senior centers; organizational characteristics; programming; awareness, attitudes, and utilization; characteristics of participants; senior center linkages with other organizations in the community services network; and policy and planning issues.

Each chapter follows the same basic format and begins with an introduction that indicates the importance of the chapter and the topics it will cover. The substantive information is then organized under five or six main topic headings. Each chapter also has a section that outlines important research questions and a chapter summary. References are provided at the end of each chapter and a subject and author index are found at the end of the book.

CHAPTER SUMMARY

Senior centers first emerged in America in the early 1940s. Since then, their number has grown to over 10,000 nationwide and the nature and scope of their activities has expanded tremendously. Yet relatively little attention has been paid to this phenomenon by gerontological researchers, and many aspects of what goes on at senior centers and who it involves are not well documented empirically.

This book strives to present a comprehensive and multifaceted analysis of senior centers in America. It focuses not only on the users of senior centers, but also on center organizational characteristics and programming. In addition, it explores the relationships senior centers have with other community organizations. The policy impact and significance of all these areas are also examined, and important research questions in each area are identified. The approach is both eclectic and holistic, and work by the author as well as other researchers and professionals is reviewed and incorporated.

Such an investigation is needed and appropriate for several reasons: the large number of senior centers and senior center users; the importance of senior centers in the aging services network and for aging policy; and the lack of availability of any similar comprehensive work. A review of the senior center literature reveals few attempts at model building but a number of alternative definitions of the term senior center. A consideration of this material suggests that a comprehensive and appropriate definition includes the following elements: a designated place; a broad array of activities and services; regular and frequent service offerings; the targeting to older people; involvement of community planning with other organizations in the community services network; and the provision of opportunities for social interaction, development of strong friendships, and the promotion of feelings of self-worth and community belonging.

Finally, although this book has not been written to examine one particular thesis or argument about senior centers, it is based on and develops a number of themes that reflect the author's research and thinking. These themes are that senior centers: generally provide a wide range of positive experiences for their users; play important roles not only in the support system of participants but also in the aging services network; cannot be fully understood without reference to larger policy issues and decisions; and must be viewed as the products of local conditions that lead to a considerable and rich diversity of form and function. However, senior centers also evidence limitations in programming, coverage, and effectiveness that must be considered in addition to the contributions they make to the elderly.

REFERENCES

Cohen, M. (1972). The multipurpose senior center. In *Senior centers: A focal point for delivery of services to older people*. Washington, DC: National Council on the Aging.

Daum, M., and Dobrof, R. (1983). Seasonal vulnerability to the old and cold: The role of the senior citizen center. *Journal of Gerontological Social Work, 5*, 81–106.

Fowler, T. (1974). Alternatives to the single site center. Washington, DC: National Council on the Aging.

Frankel, G. (1966). The multipurpose senior citizens' center: A new comprehensive agency. *The Gerontologist, 6*, 23–27.

Guttman, D., and Miller, P. (1972). Perspectives on the provision of social services in senior centers. *The Gerontologist, 12*, 403–406.

Harris, L., and Associates, Inc. (1975). *The myth and reality of aging in America*. Washington, DC: National Council on the Aging.

Jordan, J. (1978). Senior center design. An architect's discussion of facility planning. Washington, DC: National Council on the Aging.

Krout, J. (1982). Determinants of service use by the aged. Final report to the AARP Andrus Foundation. Fredonia, New York.

Krout, J. (1983a). Knowledge and use of services by the elderly: A critical review of the literature. *International Journal of Aging and Human Development, 17,* 9–23.

Krout, J. (1983b). Correlates of senior center utilization. *Research on Aging, 5,* 339–352.

Krout, J. (1983c). The organization, operation, and programming of senior centers: A national survey. Final report to the AARP Andrus Foundation. Fredonia, New York.

Krout, J. (1986). Senior center linkages in the community. *The Gerontologist, 26,* 510–515.

Krout, J. (1987). Senior center linkages and the provision of services to the elderly. Final report to the AARP Andrus Foundation. Fredonia, New York.

Krout, J. (1988). The frequency, duration, stability, and discontinuation of senior center participation: Causes and consequences. Final report to the AARP Andrus Foundation. Fredonia, New York.

Leanse, J., and Wagener, L. (1975). Senior centers: A report of senior group programs in America. Washington, DC: National Council on the Aging.

Matthews, S. (1979). *The social world of old women: Management of self-identity.* Newbury Park, CA: Sage.

Maxwell, J. (1962). Centers for older people: Guide for programs and facilities. Washington, DC: National Council on the Aging.

National Center for Health Statistics. Stone, R. (1986). Aging in the eighties, age 65 years and over—Use of community services; Preliminary data from the Supplement on Aging to the National Health Interview Survey: United States, January-June 1984. *Advance Data From Vital and Health Statistics.* No. 124, DHHS Pub. No. (PHS) 86–1250, September 30, Hyattsville, Maryland: Public Health Service.

National Institute of Senior Centers (1978). Senior center standards, guidelines for practice. Washington, DC: National Council on the Aging.

Pothier, W. (1985). Senior centers: An update before it's too late. Unpublished manuscript.

Ralston, P. (1983). Levels of senior centers: A broadened view of group based programs for the elderly. *Activities, Adaption, and Aging, 3,* 79–91.

Ralston, P. (1987). Senior center research: Policy from knowledge? In E. Borgatta and R. Montgomery (Eds.), *Critical issues in aging policy: Linking research and values.* Newbury Park, CA: Sage.

Schramm, W., and Storey, R. (1962). *Little house: A study of senior centers.* Stanford: Institute for Communication Research.

Schulder, D. (1985). Older Americans Act: A vast network of public, private agencies. *Perspective on Aging, 14,* 4–7.

Taietz, P. (1976). Two conceptual models of the senior center. *Journal of Gerontology, 31,* 219–222.

United States Senate. (1979). Older Americans Act: A staff summary. Washington, DC: U.S. Government Printing Office.

2

Growth and Development: A Historical Overview

INTRODUCTION

The purpose of this chapter is to present a historical overview of the growth and development of senior centers from their beginnings in the 1940s to the present. Important events and dates affecting senior centers nationally are identified. Much of the chapter details the impact of the three White House Conferences on Aging (WHCoA), the National Council on the Aging (NCOA), and the Older Americans Act (OAA) and its amendments for senior centers. The Older Americans Act, in particular, has had a strong impact on senior center growth and programming. Unfortunately, the diverse and rich history of senior centers at the local level simply cannot be included in this chapter. Every senior center is rooted in the efforts of key individuals and groups and has developed over the years as a result of a constellation of factors. This chapter simply attempts to provide a broad panorama of senior center growth in the last forty years to help the reader better understand their evolution into central foci for activities and services for the elderly.

THE 1940s AND 1950s: THE EARLY YEARS

It would not seem unreasonable to state that early senior centers grew out of the senior clubs that were organized for elderly people and were associated with a broad range of community organizations and community welfare agencies. Gelfand (1984) states that such clubs date back as far as 1870. It is generally recognized, however, that the first senior center, the William Hodson Community Center, was established in New York City by the Welfare Department in 1943 specifically for low-income elderly (Gelfand, 1984; Huttman, 1985). City social workers had observed that their elderly clients suffered from loneliness and isolation, and concluded they could benefit from a group setting designated specifically for older people that would provide them with the opportunity to socialize and to engage in activities of their choosing on a daily basis. This first center did not originally have programs, although they were quickly developed and a second center soon opened in another neighborhood of New York City (Lowy, 1985).

This relatively simple and straightforward idea caught on in other parts of the country. Centers were soon established by the voluntary sector in cities such as San Francisco (1947), Philadelphia (1948) and Bridgeport (1951) (Lowy, 1985). Such centers were often run with support and funds from local citizens, private welfare groups, and public agencies (Gelfand, 1984). One of the better known (and studied) early senior centers, called Little House, was established in 1949 in Menlo Park, California (Schramm and Storey, 1962). This center grew very quickly and added a large number and diversity of programs that attracted white-collar and professional participants (Maxwell, 1962).

The New York and the Menlo Park center can be seen as representing the conceptual distinction made by Taietz (1976) noted in chapter one. The New York center can be seen as the precursor to the "social agency" model, where centers are seen as providing programs to meet the needs of the elderly poor. The Menlo Park center, on the other hand, can be seen as representative of the "voluntary organization" model, in which centers are more likely to attract somewhat better off older persons who are active in voluntary organizations (Gelfand, 1984).

Several other events of note also occurred in these early years. In 1953 a description of the Hodson Center, titled *Group Work with the Aged,* was published; and the first state senior center association was started in Ohio in 1959 (Leanse, 1978). By the end of the 1950s, there were probably no more than 200 senior centers in operation across the country. These organizations were supported with local resources and sponsored by nonprofit groups or local units of government (Gelfand, 1984). No federal or state legislation existed that either funded or drew particular attention to the senior center concept.

THE 1960s: THE WHCoA AND THE OAA

By 1961, an estimated 218 senior centers were in operation in the United States. The first national directory of senior centers, developed by the National Council on the Aging five years later, identified 360, almost twice that number (Leanse, 1978). By the end of the decade, Lowy (1985) reports, this number had reached 1,058. This accelerating and inexorable growth in the number of senior centers was matched by an expansion in activities and maturation of operation, as lessons learned by older senior centers were passed on to the newer organizations.

Several events from this decade deserve mention. In 1962 the NCOA held an

"Exploratory Conference on Senior Centers," and published the first attempt at a comprehensive overview of the concept and operation of senior centers, titled *Centers for Older People: Guide for Programs and Facilities* (Leanse, 1978). A year later, the NCOA formed a National Advisory Committee on senior centers that included broad geographic and professional representation, and in 1964 NCOA convened the first annual conference of senior centers (Leanse, 1978). These conferences were held in conjunction with NCOA's annual conference, and their proceedings were published by NCOA through the 1970s.

Two other events of importance for senior centers also occurred in the 1960s. The first was the 1961 White House Conference on Aging. The impetus for this conference came from a national conference on aging held in the 1950s, and from the increasing realization among government, community and academic leaders that the nation had better begin to consider how it should respond to the growing number of Americans surviving past retirement age. While the conference delegates concerned themselves with many problems of the elderly, perhaps the issue of greatest importance for the nascent senior center movement was that of the meaningful and productive use of leisure time in retirement.

Woolf (1982) argues that the WHCoA was not important for its recognition of senior centers per se, but for the identification of activities that senior centers were already providing. Indeed, Woolf observes that the WHCoA gave more recognition to clubs than senior centers. Nonetheless, he also argues that the conference did much to promote the concept and structure of senior centers. One unfortunate outcome of the WHCoA, from Woolf's perspective, was the adoption in its report of a figure of 5 percent for the proportion of the elderly being served in "organized free-time service" (that is, senior clubs and centers) (Woolf, 1982). Woolf argues that this unsubstantiated figure severely underestimated the true amount of participation in senior centers, and that it was quoted for many years as the correct level of center usage among the elderly.

A second and more significant event was the passage of the Older Americans Act in 1965. While it is not appropriate to review in depth the history and objectives of this act—it has been amended ten times—a brief review of its purpose and several of its amendments is relevant. The Older Americans Act originally consisted of nine titles, or sections (it has since been consolidated into six), providing funds to states for research, training, and services to help older persons (Gelfand, 1984). The OAA set up a federal aging office, the Administration on Aging, and allocated money to states for providing services to the elderly. It also directed that specific service priorities be followed in the expenditure of those funds. Before long, it was amended to provide support for senior centers, which has been critical for their growth in numbers and function (Huttman, 1985). For the moment, however, the import of the original 1965 legislation will be explored.

The OAA did not include a separate section or title for senior centers or their funding. However, Section 401 (2) under Title IV (Research and Development Projects) did specify that monies could be provided by the Commissioner on

Aging for "developing or demonstrating new approaches, techniques, and methods (including the use of multipurpose activity centers) which hold promise of substantial contribution toward wholesome and meaningful living for older persons" (Lowy, 1985, 295–296). The much bigger pool of money available under Title III for program operation could not be used for construction beyond minor alterations and repairs. However, many of the programs noted under Title III, Section 301 (4), such as recreational/leisure time activities and health/welfare counseling and referral services, were provided by senior centers and could be supported by three-year grants with federal reimbursement of project costs at 75 percent, 60 percent, and 50 percent from the first to third year (Frankel, 1966). Frankel states that sponsors of the bill considered including a title in the OAA for senior center construction grants, but eliminated it for fear such a provision would impede the bill's passage.

But the Older Americans Act was not the only piece of national legislation passed in the 1960s with resource ramifications for senior centers. According to Gelfand (1984), the Public Works Development and Investment Act of 1965 made funds available that could be used for the building of multipurpose senior center facilities. The total cost of construction, renovation, and repair of buildings to be used as centers could be covered under provisions of this act. However, as with expenditures for senior centers under the OAA, data are not available on just how much money was actually used for senior centers under this legislation.

THE 1970s: EXPLOSIVE GROWTH AND CHANGE

The 1970s was a decade of great significance for senior centers in this country. Their numbers increased dramatically, and federal legislation provided more recognition and funding for their construction and operation. In fact, one could argue that this was the decade in which senior centers "came of age," becoming an accepted feature of the service network for the elderly. At least four major factors provided the impetus for this growth and maturation: the 1971 White House Conference on Aging; federal legislation, primarily 1973 and 1978 amendments to the Older Americans Act; actions by the National Council on the Aging; and increased support at the local level.

The NCOA was instrumental in providing a national forum for senior center interests, providing information about senior centers and advocating for the importance of senior centers for the elderly. Two important events occurred in 1970 involving the NCOA. The first was the formation of the National Institute of Senior Centers. This was followed in 1971 by the formation of an elected advisory committee of regional representatives, the NISC Delegate Council. The other was the publication by the NCOA of a second national directory of senior centers, containing 1,200 entries. The NISC also represented senior centers at the 1971 WHCoA. In 1972, the NISC began a national senior center newsletter called MEMO (Leanse, 1978).

In 1974, the NISC published a third national directory of senior centers and clubs, listing 5,000 organizations. Although as many as one-half of these organizations defined themselves as clubs, this has often been cited as the number of senior centers during the mid–1970s (Kent, 1978; U.S. Senate, 1979). The NISC also published a benchmark study of senior centers in 1975, titled *Senior Centers: A Report of Group Programs in America*. Funded by the Administration on Aging, this project had five objectives: compile a comprehensive, nationwide directory of senior centers and clubs; obtain basic, descriptive information on current characteristics and operations of senior centers and clubs; obtain basic information on current senior center users and nonusers and compare and contrast them; identify and describe characteristics of the optimal physical environment for senior centers; and develop a guide for senior center design and operation (Leanse and Wagener, 1975, 1). This study really was the first attempt to collect data on the varied aspects of center programming, operation, and use at a national level. Not only did it provide information of value to practitioners and policy makers of the day, the data from this project have also served as a benchmark for studies that have followed. Finally, the NISC published several other important works in the 1970s, including *Senior Center Facilities: An Architect's Evaluation* (1974), and *Senior Center Operation: A Guide to Organization and Management* (1977).

By the time the second WHCoA was held, in late 1971, senior centers had grown in number and influence and their presence was definitely a factor. Woolf (1982) observes that this conference marked a shift in the senior center movement's focus, from recreational activities to multiservice, multipurpose activities. Indeed, the conference called for the establishment of "multipurpose senior centers to provide basic social services (to include supportive, preventive, and protective), as well as link all older persons to appropriate sources of help, including home-delivered services" (Woolf, 1982, 14). The NISC itself called for such a development at the conference and requested support from the federal government.

Thus, the 1971 WHCoA marked a change in how the senior center movement saw itself, and an increased recognition on the part of others of the role senior centers should play in the aging services network. Woolf notes that the 1971 WHCoA was important for other reasons as well. First, it yielded a significant increase in the programs supported under the Older Americans Act, and in the federal monies to carry them out. Second, the 1973 amendments to the OAA can be seen as a direct result of this conference. Both the 1973 and 1978 amendments to the OAA had great impact on senior centers.

Perhaps the most important aspect of the 1973 amendments was a new Title V (now Title III) under Section 501 for "Multipurpose Senior Centers." This section defined a senior center as "a community facility for the organization and provision of a broad spectrum of services (including provision of health, social and education services and provision of facilities for recreational activities for older persons)" (OAA 1973, Sec. 5901 [c]). It also defined the center's place in the service network as "a focal point in communities for the development and delivery of social services and nutritional services" (OAA 1973, Sec. 501 [a]). The use of the term "focal point" was expanded in 1978 and, as will be seen in chapter eight, is still being explored today.

The 1973 amendments also introduced the term "multipurpose senior center" into the legislation for the first time, and "identified senior centers as a unique and separate program" (Gelfand, 1984, 139). The purpose of Title V was "to provide a focal point in communities for the development and delivery of social services and nutritional services designed primarily for older persons" (Lowy, 1985, 296). This was to be done by allocating funds for the "acquisition, alteration, or renovation" of senior centers (up to 75 percent of cost), but not for their construction or operation. This provision, however, was not funded until 1975 (Gelfand, 1984).

Several additional aspects of the 1973 amendments should be noted. Operational funds were not included under Title V, but were instead allocated for specific programs under Title III. In addition, the amendment required that multipurpose senior centers make special efforts to serve low-income and minority elderly, stating that "priority consideration will be given to facilities located in areas with high concentrations of low-income minority older persons" (Huttman, 1985).

Also of considerable significance was the creation of Area Agencies on Aging (AAAs)—community-based organizations chartered by State Units on Aging to develop comprehensive and coordinated service systems for older persons at the local level. Because senior centers were already in operation in many communities, and had built ties with local governments and the nonprofit network, it is not surprising that they would be seen as appropriate vehicles by AAAs for the provision of services as required by the OAA. Indeed, a recent analysis revealed that 41.3 percent of the grants and contracts made for the provision of services by AAAs in the early 1980s were with senior centers (National Association of State Units on Aging, 1983). The relationship between AAAs and senior centers, and the role the latter play as delivery sites, will be explored more fully in chapters seven and eight.

It has been argued that the creation of Area Agencies on Aging under the 1973 OAA amendments to administer programs drew attention and support away from senior centers. However, it is unlikely that senior centers would have been capable of developing and operating all the varied services funded by OAA legislation—especially as priority services and target groups changed through further amendments. A focus on services such as in-home, and on target groups such as the low-income and frail, might well have jeopardized some of the very aspects of senior centers responsible for their success in the first place. These issues will be explored more fully, as well, in chapter eight.

The effect of the 1973 legislation on the numbers of senior centers and their operation was immediate. Estes (1980) reports that by 1977, the Administration on Aging was supporting nearly 1,500 senior centers to the amount of $20 million, with appropriations set for $40 million in 1978. But it is important to note that financial support for centers came from other federal programs as well. Title XX of the Social Security Act, for example, initiated in 1974, allocated funds for social services for low-income persons that could be used to support programs at senior centers. The use of these funds has been problematic, because programs operated with OAA monies have only age requirements, none for income. The Housing and Community Development Act of 1974 also provided money for construction funds related to community services, primarily for lower and moderate income people (Gelfand, 1984). This program is also known as Community Block Grants. While these programs no doubt played a role in the growth of senior centers in the 1970s, it is very difficult to determine accurately the relative importance of each, as the dollar amounts going to senior centers under each program are hard to identify.

The Older Americans Act was amended again in 1978, with important ramifications for senior centers. As part of these amendments, Title V was consolidated under Title III, which now included social services, nutrition, and multipurpose senior centers. Title III now could "provide for acquisition, alteration, renovation, or construction of facilities for multiple purpose senior centers as well as provide for the operations of these centers" (Gelfand, 1984, 139). However, this also meant that no monies would specifically be earmarked for senior centers. In fact, only in 1977 and 1978 were separate appropriations made for senior centers (Lowy, 1985). Senior centers would not have to compete with other organizations for Title III program monies, or for non-OAA federal dollars. One result of this has been that senior center programming funded by the OAA has had to conform to federal Administration on Aging and Area Agency on Aging standards in order to receive OAA monies. Moreover, states are required to spend at least half of Title III money on access, in-home, and legal services (Lowy, 1985). Another consequence, as will be demonstrated in the next chapter, is that senior centers rely on non-OAA funding to a considerable degree. Reauthorization of the OAA in 1981, 1984, and most recently 1987 did not basically change the provisions under Title III.

The 1978 amendments included other language relevant to senior centers. This was the requirement that Area Agencies on Aging designate, where feasible, a "focal point" for the comprehensive and coordinated delivery of services to the elderly called for in the 1973 legislation. It was further stated that multipurpose senior centers be given "special consideration" as focal points (Sec. 306 [a] ; Wagener, 1981). As a result, most senior centers have been designated by AAAs as focal points. Wagener (1981) reports that a survey of AAAs revealed that 64 percent of the agencies designated as focal points were senior centers. A more recent study by the author (Krout, 1987) revealed that 74 percent of the senior centers in a nationally representative sample indicated designation by an AAA as a focal point. Considerable attention will be given to the focal point roles played by senior centers in chapter eight. This concept and the importance of senior centers as suitable focal points have certainly contributed to their visibility and importance.

What was the impact of these legislative changes on senior centers in the 1970s? It is clear that the increased funding did much to accelerate the establishment of new centers, to speed the evolution of many organizations into true multipurpose centers, and to increase their visibility and recognition in the community. The NCOA study referred to in the previous section found that 17 percent of the senior centers in their survey were established before 1965, 32 percent between 1965 and 1969, and 51 percent between 1970 and 1973. The percentages for multipurpose versus regular senior centers were almost identical. These figures indicate that the growth in senior centers was surging in the late 1960s and early 1970s, before the 1973 OAA amendments. The author's study of a small national sample of centers found that 20 percent of the centers studied were established before 1970, 40 percent between 1970 and 1975, 30 percent between 1976 and 1980, and 10 percent after 1980. These figures support the thesis that the 1970s was a time of considerable center expansion. However, there are problems of interpretation here, as some centers may trace their roots back to club or organizational status, thus identifying their date of origin differently.

THE 1980s: SLOWING GROWTH AND EXPANDING FUNCTIONS

It would appear that by the end of the 1970s the number of senior centers in America was probably around 6,000 to 7,000. Woolf (1982) states that 8,000 centers were in operation by the early 1980s, and Schulder (1985) reports a figure of 10,000. By the late 1980s, the mailing list of the NCOA included almost 18,000 senior centers and clubs, of which it is reasonable to argue that at least 10,000 are senior centers by most commonly used definitions. These data suggest that while the 1980s witnessed only modest growth in the number of senior centers, the breadth and depth of services offered by them has increased significantly in the wake of the 1978 amendments to the OAA.

This development is also reflected in the increased number of centers that identify themselves as multipurpose. Data collected in late 1984 in a national survey of senior centers and clubs revealed that 82 percent of the centers identified themselves as multipurpose (Sela, 1986), while 74 percent of a small national random sample of senior centers studied by the author in 1986 claimed multipurpose status (Krout, 1987). Since these studies used different sampling methodologies, it is not clear if there is a significant difference between them. In addition, the designation of multipurpose, especially as it is often self-proclaimed, it is not clear and presents problems in interpretation. However, the data would seem to indicate that there has been a considerable increase in the percentage of multipurpose senior centers in the last decade.

The third WHCoA was held in 1981, and was dominated by what some in

the gerontological community saw as attempts by the new political administration
to de-emphasize the problems of the elderly and to lessen the federal commitment
to providing resources to meet those needs (Oriol, 1983). An analysis of the
outcome of this conference will not be attempted here. However, it would appear
that this conference did not have significant impact on the senior center concept
or on government policy towards senior centers. This is not to say that senior
centers were disparaged at the conference. Indeed, the 1981 WHCoA "mini-
conference" on senior centers stated:

over the years, senior centers—community based and supported—have demonstrated their
ability to enhance the physical, social, and emotional well-being of large numbers of
older persons. Today the senior center is a community focal point—a gathering place for
older persons and a vehicle through which they can access a broad range of services that
addresses their needs with dignity and respect, supports their capacity to grow and develop,
and facilitates their continued involvement in the community. (U.S. Government Printing
Office, 1981, 1)

In addition, the mini-conference report made fifteen recommendations in support
of senior centers. Many of these recommendations called for strengthening and
expanding existing recognition of and federal funding for senior centers. They
covered items such as:

—focal point status
—funding for services in congregate settings
—financial support for volunteers
—funding for preventive and restorative health services
—long term care services
—coordination with other components of service delivery system

The 1981 WHCoA final report resolved that a multipurpose senior center be
located in each community through:

—pooling federal, state, and local funds for new construction, or expansion and rehabilitation of existing structures
—locating or co-locating needed services in such centers
—assuring that all services and programs are free from physical and language barriers
  (WCoA, 1982).

Despite all these recommendations, it would not appear that the federal commitment to senior centers increased in the 1980s. Indeed, funding for Title III
remained flat, and the basic thrust of federal policy in the 1980s was a decrease
in support for many social programs.

The Older Americans Act was amended three times in the 1980s (1981, 1984,

1987) and it would appear that none of these amendments significantly changed the status of senior centers in this legislation. The 1984 amendments did create a new Title VII, Personal Health Education and Training Programs for Older Individuals. This title authorized discretionary grants and contracts with colleges and universities for designing health education and training programs for multipurpose senior centers. However, no money has been set aside for this title. Funding has continued to be allocated under Title III to states, and from states to local Area Agencies on Aging for services.

Federal priorities under the OAA have shifted, and funding for Title III has witnessed relatively little growth in the 1980s (Binstock, 1987). One result has been that the monies available to AAAs to fund programs at senior centers have shrunk in relation to the number of potential service recipients nationwide. Other changes in federal legislation (for example, the amending of Title XX of the Social Security Act with the Social Service Block Grant) have resulted in reduced federal outlays for services for the elderly (Oriol, 1983). In addition, the competition for available dollars has increased as more organizations, including for-profit ones, have entered the aging services business. Senior centers then, will likely continue to see the federal share of their funding shrink.

It is useful to examine closely the 1987 amendments to the OAA to get a clear picture of the role seen for senior centers in that legislation in the late 1980s. References to multipurpose senior centers (the term "senior center" alone does not appear in the act) can be found in Title II and in at least a dozen places in Title III (U.S. Department of Health and Human Services, 1987). Significantly, Title II, Section 207 (b) calls for the Commissioner of Aging to report to Congress by January 1990 on the national unmet need for supportive and nutritional services and for multipurpose senior centers. The information is to be collected from the states. This requirement that states determine unmet need for multipurpose senior centers is one new aspect of the 1987 amendments.

As indicated above, reference to multipurpose senior centers in the OAA is largely concentrated in Title III. In describing the purpose of Title III, Section 301 (a) identifies multipurpose senior centers as one of the services the act is intended to design and support. Section 302 (10) defines multipurpose senior centers as a "community facility for the organization and provision of a broad spectrum of services, which shall include, but not be limited to, provision of health (including mental health), social, nutritional, and educational services and the provision of facilities for recreational activities for older individuals."

Section 306 (a) (1) concerns Area Agency on Aging plans. It specifies that such plans shall provide for "where appropriate, the establishment, maintenance or construction of multipurpose senior centers," determine the need for them and other services and "enter into agreements with . . . multipurpose senior centers for the provision of such services or centers" to meet needs in the area. As in previous amendments, Area Agency plans are instructed to identify focal points, "giving special consideration to designating multipurpose senior centers as such" (Section 306 [a] [3]), and to provide "appropriate technical assistance" to service providers such as multipurpose senior centers (Section 306 [a] [6] [B]). The section on state plans requires that states evaluate the need for multipurpose senior centers, and that they give "particular attention" to using multipurpose senior centers for congregate meal sites (Section 307 [a] [3] [A], [13] [D]).

Part B of Title III, Supportive Services and Senior Centers, identifies the types of service for which grants will be made to states. As in previous amendments, Section 321 (6) (1) indicates that grants will be made to states for purchasing or renovating existing facilities and for constructing new facilities to serve as multipurpose senior centers. Section 321 (6) (2) states that funds may also be used to pay for operating costs. However, it should be stressed that such language does not guarantee senior centers will receive OAA monies. There is tremendous variation at the state and local level in the allocation of funds for the construction, renovation, and operation of senior centers.

Despite the prominence of multipurpose senior centers in the language of the Older Americans Act, the legislation does not designate funding specifically for their construction or operation. The $399 million authorized under Title III-B for 1989 by the 1987 amendments is for a wide range of services. Nutrition programs are funded separately by Title III-C. Certainly, senior centers do receive monies under Title III for providing these services, but it is virtually impossible to state exactly how much federal, state, and local money goes towards supporting senior center operation and programs.

RESEARCH QUESTIONS

Overall, very little has been written on the history of senior centers in the United States. Thus, the factors responsible for their emergence and growth are not well documented or understood. This chapter has focused on the importance of the WHCoAs, the National Council on the Aging, and the Older Americans Act. But these phenomena are only a part of the story. What events occurred at the local and state level over the years to account for senior center expansion? It is reasonable to state that grass-roots organizing by seniors and social service professionals played an important role, but how important a role, and of what kind? Much of this information is probably known by persons involved with individual senior centers, by aging network professionals, such as AAA staff, who worked to help establish or expand these organizations. Yet these stories are largely untold.

It would seem appropriate to call for a much greater research emphasis in this area. It is very convenient, but not particularly insightful, to say that the senior center expansion of the 1960s and 1970s was intertwined with the demographic, political, and social events of the time. The author is not an historian, and would certainly not contend that the discussion contained in this chapter is adequate. It is only a beginning. The bulk of this book is concerned with what senior centers are today—with some attention to where they have been and where they might be going. The data available on senior centers in the 1950s and 1960s are sparse indeed, with somewhat more information collected during the 1970s and 1980s. But the existing research rarely involves an examination of historical processes as they have affected senior centers. An idea of the change senior centers have experienced can be obtained by comparing studies conducted at different points in time. However, the comparison of findings from cross-sectional studies has numerous drawbacks and is not a substitute for longitudinal research or historical analysis.

CHAPTER SUMMARY

This chapter has presented an overview of the growth, expansion, and development of senior centers in the United States. From rather humble beginnings in the 1940s, senior centers have grown to be some 10,000 or more strong. Three White House Conferences on Aging, the passage of the Older Americans Act in 1965 and subsequent amendments, and the activities of the National Council on the Aging have played important roles in this growth and expansion.

The NCOA held one of the first, if not the first, conference on senior centers in 1962. In the 1970s, NCOA increased its activity in the senior center field by publishing directories and resource materials, conducting a landmark national study, and establishing the National Institute of Senior Centers. The NISC serves as an advocate for senior centers at the national level and as a source of technical information for senior centers across the nation. The first WHCoA (1961) drew attention not to senior centers themselves, but to the activities and services needed by the elderly that the small number of existing senior centers were already providing. The 1971 WHCoA heightened the visibility of senior centers and called for their establishment as multipurpose service sites.

The 1971 WHCoA also provided a significant impetus for the expansion of the Older Americans Act. Passed in 1965, this legislation had significant ramifications for senior centers nationwide. The OAA specifically identified senior centers as appropriate vehicles for the development and delivery of support services to the elderly, and authorized monies for the services senior centers provided. In the 1970s, the OAA was amended to allow money to be used for senior center construction and operation. The term multipurpose senior center was introduced into the legislation, and senior centers were defined as playing a "focal point" role in the community-based service system. It should also be noted that by setting up the system of State Units on Aging and Area Agencies on Aging, amendments to the OAA have been seen by some as de-emphasizing the importance of senior centers in the aging services network. Indeed, subsequent amendments have called for the increased targeting of services to groups such as low-income, minority, and frail persons, that many senior centers would seem to serve in limited numbers. But overall, it would appear that the resources provided to senior centers under the OAA have stimulated rather than hindered their growth and development.

The 1980s did not produce the watershed events for senior centers that occurred in previous decades. The 1981 WHCoA, embroiled as it was for a time in political controversy, produced little of consequence for senior centers, nor did the 1981, 1984, and 1987 amendments to the Older Americans Act. However, the increasing breadth of service needs recognized and addressed by this legislation has played an important role in the continued evolution of senior centers as multipurpose focal points. This statement must be tempered by the observation that the Reagan years were not generally beneficial to the aging services network. Subsequently, the competition for program dollars has become even more fierce, and the absolute amount of funding available at all levels of government for senior center operation and programming has not kept pace with the demand or need for services.

REFERENCES

Binstock, R. (1987). Title III of the Older Americans Act: An analysis and proposal for the 1987 Reauthorization. *The Gerontologist, 27,* 259–265.

Estes, C. (1980). *The aging enterprise.* San Francisco: Jossey-Bass Publishers.

Frankel, G. (1966). The multipurpose senior citizens' center: A new comprehensive agency. *The Gerontologist, 6,* 23–27.

Gelfand, D. (1984). *The aging network: Programs and services.* New York: Springer Publishing Company.

Huttman, E. (1985). *Social services for the elderly.* New York: Free Press.

Kent, D. (1978). The how and why of senior centers. *Aging,* May/June, 2–6.

Krout, J. (1987). Senior center linkages and the provision of services to the elderly. Final report to the AARP Andrus Foundation. Fredonia, New York.

Leanse, J. (1978). A blend of multi-dimensional activities. *Perspective on Aging, 7,* March/April, 8–13.

Leanse, J., and Wagener, L. (1975). Senior centers: A report of senior group programs in America. Washington, DC: National Council on the Aging.

Lowy, L. (1985). Multipurpose senior centers. In A. Monk (Ed.), *Handbook of gerontological services.* New York: Van Nostrand Reinhold Co.

Maxwell, J. (1962). Centers for older people: Guide for programs and facilities. Washington, DC: National Council on the Aging.

National Association of State Units on Aging. (1983). A profile of state and area agencies on aging (1981). Washington, DC.

Oriol, W. (1983). New directions or old themes revisited? The present federal role in service entitlements. *The Gerontologist, 23,* 399–401.

Schramm, W., and Storey, R. (1962). *Little House: A study of senior centers.* Stanford: Institute for Communication Research.

Schulder, D. (1985). Older Americans Act: A vast network of public, private agencies. *Perspective on Aging, 14,* 4–7.

Sela, I. (1986). A study of programs and services for the hearing impaired elderly in senior centers and clubs in the U.S. Unpublished dissertation. Washington, DC: Gallaudet College.

Taietz, P. (1976). Two conceptual models of the senior center. *Journal of Gerontology, 31,* 219–222.

United States Department of Health and Human Services. (1987). Older Americans Act of 1965, Washington, DC.

United States Government Printing Office. (1981). 1981 White House Conference on Aging: Report of the mini-conference on senior centers. Washington, DC.

United States Senate. (1979). Older Americans Act: A staff summary. Washington, DC: U.S. Government Printing Office.

Wagener, L. (1981). The senior center: A partner in the community care system. Washington, DC: National Council on the Aging.

White House Conference on Aging. (1982). Final report: The 1981 White House Conference on Aging. 3 Vols. Washington, DC: The Conference.

Woolf, L. (1982). How senior centers grew through three WHCoAs. *Perspective on Aging, 11,* 13–17.

3

Organizational Characteristics

INTRODUCTION

This chapter focuses on the organizational aspects of senior centers. Topics covered include philosophy and goals, organization type, facilities, budget and budget source, and staffing patterns (including director characteristics). In addition, the concept of "linkage" with other organizations is introduced. A consideration of these topics lays the foundation for further examination of what senior centers are and do. While it might appear obvious that the organizational and resource bases of senior centers are key ingredients in center programming and operation, little systematic attention has been paid to these topics by researchers (Krout, 1984). In fact, most studies omit altogether a consideration of their role. Many of the organizational and resource variables discussed here will be considered in other chapters as well because they are so closely related to other aspects of senior centers, especially programming and participation issues.

PHILOSOPHY AND GOALS

A number of fundamental assumptions about aging and the aged appear to lie at the heart of the senior center concept. These can be seen as based on an "activity" versus a "disengagement" theory of aging. Seniors are seen as valued members of society, capable of personal growth and in need of opportunities for social interaction and community involvement. The National Institute of Senior Centers' philosophy is as follows:

A senior center seeks to create an atmosphere that acknowledges the value of human life, individually and collectively, and affirms the dignity and self-worth of the older adult.

This atmosphere provides for the reaffirmation of creative potential, the power of decision making, the skills of coping and defending, the warmth of caring, sharing, giving and supporting. The uniqueness of the senior center stems from its total concern for older people and its concern for the total older person. In an atmosphere of wellness, it develops strengths and encourages independence, while building interdependence and supporting unavoidable dependencies. It works with older persons, not for them enabling and facilitating their decisions and actions, and in so doing creates and supports a sense of community that further enables older persons to continue their involvement with and contribution to the larger community.

The philosophy of the senior-center movement is based on the premises that aging is a normal developmental process; that human beings need peers with whom they can interact and who are available as a source of encouragement and support; and that adults have the right to have a voice in determining matters in which they have a vital interest (National Institute of Senior Centers, 1978, 5).

Philosophies such as this are reflected somewhat more concretely through the goals pursued by organizations or their members. A goal can be seen as a purpose or end result that is strived for. Goals are basic to individual and group behavior. People have goals that help direct how they act in their daily lives. Groups, formal and informal, also have goals that relate to what the group or organization hopes to achieve. Informal groups such as play groups of children (or adults) often do not have explicit, written, or even verbally acknowledged goals, whereas more formally constituted groups, such as senior centers, often do. Thus, social scientists look at the goals of a group or organization to understand its actions. While a fair amount has been written about the ideal goals and purposes of senior centers, little has been reported on what those goals and purposes actually are.

Recall that two of the five definitions reviewed in chapter one included a statement about purposes or goals. Maxwell (1962, 7) notes that the purpose of senior centers is to "provide older people with socially enriching experiences which would help preserve their dignity as human beings and enhance their feelings of self-worth." In addition to this focus on the value of the self, the National Institute of Senior Centers (1978, 15) definition states that senior centers encourage older persons "involvement in and with the community." This reflects the NISC's view of senior centers as community focal points that serve as a bridge or link between older persons and the larger community. The idea of involving the older person beyond the activities at a center reflects a more other-directed notion of the purposes of senior centers.

Cohen (1972, 3–4) notes that senior centers provide the following benefits for the individual:

1. Meaningful individual and group relationships
2. Learning new skills for personal enrichment in the arts, languages, music, dramatics, nature, sports and games, dance, and crafts
3. Being useful and helpful to others through volunteer community services
4. Assisting a person to maintain physical strength

5. Promoting mental health through the use and development of creative abilities

6. Developing a valued role in society

7. Helping the individual to keep informed about changes in the community and the world

8. Developing an individual's group-leadership skills and personal effectiveness in dealing with others

9. Information and consultation on personal problems

For the family, senior centers are to offer opportunities for:

1. Developing new skills and experiences to share with family members

2. Helping older persons to be less dependent on family for activity and interests and not totally dependent on family relationships for emotional support

3. Helping the individual continue to contribute to the family's emotional well-being

For the community, senior centers are to offer opportunities for:

1. Helping older people to remain in the community by assisting them to maintain their emotional well-being

2. Helping the community to be aware of the total needs of its older citizens, pointing up gaps and needed services

3. Providing a resource of volunteer manpower from among the membership group for public and private nonprofit community agencies and organizations

These statements reflect what observers of the gerontological scene feel senior centers should do. Perhaps of greater importance are the goal statements drawn up for senior centers by their board of directors or expressed by senior center staff. Several studies with nationally representative samples provide some insight into this issue. For example, the NCOA's national survey carried out in the early 1970s asked senior center directors the degree to which they felt their programs worked towards ten different goals. Two-thirds responded that they agreed "strongly" or "very strongly" that senior center programs foster independence, use capabilities of the participants, and promote self-help, while 40 percent responded similarly that senior programs promote self-government (Leanse and Wagener, 1975).

The author's own study (Krout, 1987) provides more in-depth data on center goals, using a national sample of some 250 senior centers. Center directors were asked if they had a goal statement and if so, to give a brief description of that statement. Seventy percent of the survey respondents said they did have a goal statement for their center. Data reported in Table 3.1 show that over 40 percent said their main goal was in the area of service provision, with recreation, health, and nutrition services most frequently mentioned. Expanding the numbers of elderly served was also mentioned by a considerable number of center directors.

Table 3.1
Senior Center Goals

| Goal | Percent of Respondents* | | |
	First Goal	Second Goal	Third Goal
Education			
Education in general	5	10	8
Nutrition education	–	–	1
Education Total	5	10	9
Services			
Services in general	16	21	16
Health services	3	3	3
Nutrition services	8	8	4
Expand services	2	1	–
Expand number of elderly served	4	–	4
Recreation services	9	6	8
Services for frail	1	3	4
Increase access to services	–	1	–
Home services	1	4	1
Services Total	44	47	40
Independence/Quality of Life			
Image/self worth in general	1	1	4
Train/encourage elderly to volunteer in community	1	3	4
Maintain independence of elderly	15	6	5
Increase public awareness/ image/relations	–	–	5
Improve image of aging	1	1	1
Promote friendship	6	7	3
Increase quality of life/ dignity	9	8	3
Increase senior involvement in center/community	2	5	3
Increase income/buying power	–	–	3
Independence/Quality of Life Total	35	31	31
Referral/Linkages			
Referrals/linkages in general	–	–	1
Identify informal services providers	1	1	–
Identify formal service providers	1	1	–
Work with health services	–	–	1
Increase/better referrals & information to elderly	2	3	4

Table 3.1 (continued)

Goal	First Goal	Percent of Respondents* Second Goal	Third Goal
Provide information on services– (own & others)		–	5
Meet/work/coordinate with service providers	1	1	3
Referral/linkages total	5	6	14
Other			
General	1	2	1
Outreach especially to home– bound/ill	1	3	1
Advocate for senior rights	–	1	1
Focal point	5	–	–
Purchase/upgrade building/ equipment	2	1	1
Needs assessment	2	1	–
Decreased funds/programs/ agencies	1	–	–
Transportation/escort services	2	1	4
Others Total	14	9	8

*N = 246

Source: J. Krout (1987).   Senior center linkages and the provision of services to the elderly. Final report to the AARP Andrus Foundation. Fredonia, N.Y.

Thirty-five percent said their major emphasis was in the area of seniors' self worth and image, while 15 percent indicated that maintaining the independence of the elderly was most important. Promoting friendship and increasing the quality and dignity of life were also frequently mentioned in this area. Five percent said education was their major goal and another five percent stated referrals and linkages were their main objective. Fourteen percent gave other goals such as upgrading buildings and equipment, outreach to homebound, transportation, and functioning better as a focal point. Similar breakdowns can be seen for the second and third priority goals. These data indicate that providing services and activities to the elderly and increasing their independence and quality of life are the dominant goals noted by senior center directors. Several of the components found in the definition of senior centers in chapter one, such as the focal point role and community linkage, are not widely recognized in the goal priorities of center directors.

ORGANIZATIONAL TYPE

Senior centers vary on a number of organizational characteristics and one of the most important is whether or not they are classified as "muiltipurpose." A multipurpose senior center can be viewed as more complex than an ordinary senior center, as it provides a wider range of activities and services for participants as well as for those who may come to the center sporadically for special programs or use it as an information source. Maxwell (1962) also notes that multipurpose senior centers need a larger number of staff with diversified skills.

Data from the author's 1987 project, listed in Table 3.2, show that 74 percent of the senior centers in the sample classified themselves as multipurpose, 14 percent as senior centers, 10 percent as nutrition sites, and 2 percent as "other." The percentage for multipurpose is significantly higher than the 29 percent reported by Leanse and Wagener (1975) for the early 1970s. This increase likely reflects the growth in senior center numbers and scope of activity brought about by the amendments to the Older Americans Act in the 1970s, the greater resources (at least initially) and visibility these amendments brought to senior centers, and the continued support of the senior center concept at the local level.

Another important organizational characteristic is whether a senior center is a freestanding entity or is subsumed under a larger organization. Senior centers may function as part of a program or as a unit of public agencies such as state or local departments of recreation, social services, health, or education. They may also be sponsored by private, nonprofit organizations. The author's two recent national studies (Krout, 1983, 1987) found an almost identical 66 percent and 65 percent of senior centers identified as a subunit of another organization. As can be seen in Table 3.2, the 1987 study found almost 40 percent of the centers were subunits of AAAs, 17 percent to 18 percent were part of park and recreation departments, of not-for-profit organizations and of other agencies, and 8 percent were affiliated with councils on aging. In addition, data presented in Table 3.2 show that three-quarters of the centers that were subunits of other agencies were not the only senior center administered by that agency. Almost 30 percent indicated that the number of other centers covered was greater than five.

Two other pieces of information on senior centers are presented in Table 3.2. The first is that the senior centers in the study had been in operation for a mean of twelve years. Since the data were collected in 1986, the average year the centers began operation was 1974. One-fifth of the centers reported being established before 1970, and two-fifths from 1971 to 1975. Another 30 percent initiated activity between 1976 and 1980. The second piece of information is that three-quarters of the senior centers reported being open five days a week, presumably Monday through Friday. Ten percent of the sample reported being open less than five days, and one in eight more than five days a week. In contrast, data reported from a study in the early 1960s of several hundred senior centers revealed that the majority of centers were open only two days a week in those early days (Maxwell, 1962).

FACILITIES

The nature and adequacy of the physical facility in which a senior center is located significantly affects its ability to attract participants and to meet their

Table 3.2
General Characteristics of Senior Centers

Characteristic	Percent*
Center Type	
Multipurpose senior center	73.9
Senior center	13.5
Nutrition program/site	10.2
Other	2.4
Subunit Status	
Yes	64.9
No	35.1
Subunit of What Agency	
AAA	38.2
Council on Aging	8.3
Park & Recreation	17.2
Not for profit	18.5
Other	17.8
Number of Other Centers	
none	23.0
1	15.0
2	8.0
3	8.0
4	8.0
5	9.0
more than 5	29.0
Mean	7.2
Median	3.0
Number of Years in Operation	
1 - 5	10.4
6 - 10	30.3
11 - 15	39.8
16 or more	19.5
Mean	12.4
Median	11.5
Number of Days Open Per Week	
2, 3, 4	10.6
5	76.7
6, 7	12.6
Mean	4.9
Median	5.0

*N=246

Source: J. Krout (1987). Senior center linkages and the provision of services to the elderly. Final report to the AARP Andrus Foundation. Fredonia, N.Y.

programming needs and interests. Ideally, senior centers should be located in attractive buildings in neighborhoods that are convenient to transportation and parking. They should also be handicapped accessible and have an interior space that can accomodate varied activities. Indeed, the importance of senior center facilities is reflected by the fact that the original Title V of the OAA authorized monies exclusively for senior center facility building and renovation.

Because senior centers have origins in diverse organizations and communities, and because the amount of funding for building renovation and new construction has varied over time, the facilities in which senior centers are found take many shapes indeed. For example, senior centers included in a recent study conducted by the author were housed in facilities as diverse as an old house, a fire hall, a renovated machine shop, an elementary school, and a community center, as well as in several buildings built specifically to be a center (Krout, 1988). In the early 1970s, only one-quarter of senior centers were located in a separate building used solely for that purpose. Another one-quarter were housed in recreation or community centers, while 17 percent reported a location in a church or synagogue, 10 percent were located in senior housing authority buildings, 15 percent operated from a local or county government facility, and 18 percent had other arrangements. Four of ten centers reported that they were located in renovated facilities, while a little more than one-third used old buildings not renovated for senior center use. Only 20 percent were in new buildings (Leanse and Wagener, 1975).

By the mid–1980s, however, a much larger percentage of senior centers were located in a separate facility. Data from the author's recent study show slightly more than one-half of centers were located in a separate facility (Krout, 1987). Fifteen percent were housed in a recreation or community center, while 10 percent were in a multiservice agency. Finally, a total of 22 percent were found in an assortment of other places, such as religious organizations, housing projects, and schools. This doubling of the percentage located in separate buildings is an important development, and can be seen as both a cause and consequence of the increase in the importance and visibility of senior centers.

Another aspect of the facility is its size. Here a trend over the years to larger and single-story buildings can be observed. For example, the mean and median square footage of senior centers in the author's 1987 study were 7,549 and 4,801 respectively (Krout, 1987). These numbers are considerably larger than those reported in the early 1970s (Leanse and Wagener, 1975). Also at that time, two-thirds of the senior center buildings were single-level facilities (Leanse and Wagener, 1975), but by the mid–1980s this proportion had risen to four in five (Krout, 1987). The increase in square footage, new construction, and single-story buildings appears to be related to a reduction in the number of senior center facilities seen as inadequate by center directors. The NCOA study (Leanse and Wagener, 1975) reported that 26 percent of center directors felt the center facility greatly limited the kind and number of programs offered, while this figure dropped to 16 percent by the early 1980s (Krout, 1984). However, while facilities have evidently improved, some problems are still reported to exist, especially in the areas of handicapped access, kitchen space, and common space such as dining and recreation areas (Krout, 1983).

The author's national survey taken in the early 1980s reveals variation in facilities based on census region and community size. For example, senior centers in the Northeast were least likely to be located in separate facilities, perhaps because of the availability of older, multistory buildings and the relative lack of new construction in the 1970s. Centers in this region were also found to be considerably smaller than those in other areas, and almost twice as likely to be located in buildings with two or more floors (Krout, 1984). Differences based on community size also exist. Senior centers located in the central cities of metropolitan areas, for example, are much less likely to be located in separate facilities, perhaps because they are much more likely to be a subunit of another organization and thus share space with that organization. Not surprisingly, senior center size, as measured by square footage, increases dramatically as one moves up the urbanization scale: central city centers are two and one-half times larger than their rural counterparts (Krout, 1984). It is interesting to note that despite the apparent building size and type disadvantages found in the Northeast and in rural communities, no significant differences are found for perceived limitations of facilities based on region or degree of urbanization (Krout, 1984).

BUDGET SIZE AND SOURCES

Central to the operation of any organization are its financial resources. This section considers what is known about the budgets of senior centers and where their financial resources come from. Data from the last twenty years indicate that there has been a steady growth, even when inflation is taken into account, in the size of senior center budgets. The average senior center budget increased from $17,650 in 1968 to $36,200 in 1973, and $50,000 in 1974 (Lowy, 1985). By 1982, four of ten senior centers reported budgets greater than $50,000 (Krout, 1984). By 1986, as shown in Table 3.3, the author found a mean budget of $121,000, with six of ten centers reporting budgets of $50,000 and up (Krout, 1987). While the comparability of these figures may suffer due to the different samples on which they are based, the trend is unmistakable. The relative degree to which federal, state, and local expenditures have accounted for this increase is not known.

Senior centers rarely receive all of their funding from one source, and they generally utilize a variety of sources for different aspects of center operation and programming (administration, rent and utilities, congregate meals, transportation, and so on). An examination of data on budget sources in Table 3.3 reveals the nature of some of this diversity. The five largest categories are federal (29 percent), city (25 percent), fund-raising (14 percent), state (12 percent) and

Table 3.3
Senior Center Budget and Budget Sources

Budget Variable	Percent*
Budget	
Less than $25,000	26.0
$25,000 - $49,999	17.0
$50,000 - $99,999	22.0
$100,000 - $249,999	17.0
$250,000 and up	13.0
Mean	$121,157
Median	$ 56,950
Budget Source	
Federal (includes pass through)	28.8
State	11.7
County	9.1
City	24.7
Dues	1.5
Fund raising	13.5
Meal contribution	3.2
Other	7.5
In-Kind Dollar Value	
None	15.0
Less than $2,000	12.0
$2,000 - 4,999	17.0
$5,000 - 9,999	12.0
$10,000 - 19,999	18.0
$20,000 - 39,999	13.0
Mean	$ 22,357
Median	$ 8,101
In-Kind Sources	
Federal/state	7.1
City/county/town	23.0
Private	20.9
Volunteer hours	16.7

*N = 246
Source: J. Krout (1987). Senior center linkages and the provision of
          services to the elderly. Final report to the AARP Andrus
          Foundation. Fredonia, New York.

county (9 percent). Since significant amounts of the state, city, and county dollars could in fact be federal, the true contribution from this source is hard to gauge. Gross expenditures for senior centers at the federal level are hard to pin down as well, because dollars are reported by program, not by delivery site.

Gelfand (1984) notes a number of potential federal funding sources for senior centers. Several parts of the OAA can be utilized. These include Title III, for construction, operation, nutrition services and special programming; Title IV, for training and research and for model projects; and Title V, for senior community service employment programs. Other federal sources include Community Development Block Grants, ACTION for personnel resources, and Social Services block grants. Senior centers may receive state funding for operations through legislative appropriations, or through state agency funds for programs and services. Funding is also received from civic and religious organizations, as well as local governmental units. In addition, senior centers may often receive in-kind contributions, such as facility space and maintenance, supplies, and personnel. Finally, senior centers also generate income through donations, membership dues, and fund-raising activities.

An additional comment on in-kind contributions seems appropriate, as this source has rarely been given much more than passing mention. Table 3.3 shows a wide range of in-kind contributions. While 15 percent of the centers reported no in-kind contributions, 13 percent reported $20,000 or greater. The mean was $22,000, but the median only $8,000. Local governments, private organizations, and the dollar value of volunteer hours were the largest sources of these in-kind contributions. Most frequently, these contributions involve the use of facilities and equipment at zero or minimal cost. However, the value of volunteer labor may well be underestimated (Krout, 1987).

Data in Table 3.3 also reveal a considerable amount of variation in senior center budgets. Size of budget can be expected to influence both the quantity and quality of program offerings and operation. Significant geographic variations exist in budget size as well. Research by the author has shown, for example, a very strong relationship between size of community in which a center is located and senior center budget (Krout, 1984, 1987). While 42 percent of the centers located in rural communities reported budgets of less than $10,000, only 17 percent of central city and 16 percent of suburban centers reported the same low amount. On the other hand, 43 percent of the central city, as opposed to 8 percent of the rural centers, noted budgets of $75,000 or more. These differences are dramatic indeed. Community size differences are reflected in budget sources as well. Rural centers receive a much greater proportion of their budget from federal and county sources, and a much smaller proportion from city government and private sources (Krout, 1984). Rural centers receive 36 percent of their monies from federal, 15 percent from city, and 14 percent from county governments. Central city centers, on the other hand, get 23 percent from federal, 31 percent from city, and 9 percent from county governments (Krout, 1987).

The possible impact of these community size differences on senior center budgets and on center programming is indeed important. It is appropriate, as well, to consider their cause. The author has argued elsewhere that the rural disadvantage can be seen as a result of the generally lower levels of income and expenditures for many types of services in rural areas (Krout, 1984). Kim (1981) has argued forcefully that government programs at all levels systematically discriminate against the rural elderly, leaving fewer dollars for the operation of programs such as nutrition and recreation at rural senior centers. The fact that the federal share is higher for rural centers may simply reflect the absence of city governments and the smaller amount of local resources available to organizations. Several other explanations should be noted. One is that senior center budgets in rural areas are lower because the number of center users is much smaller, as is the demand for services, based on size and density of population. However, as pointed out by the author and others (Krout, 1986a), strong arguments can be made for higher levels of need as well as higher service delivery costs in rural areas.

STAFFING PATTERNS

Senior center staffing patterns have important ramifications for many aspects of senior center operation. The number and qualifications of staff can clearly affect the quantity, quality, and diversity of center programming. Given the growth in senior center budgets and emergence of senior centers as an important component of the service delivery network over the years, it seems logical to expect that the number of staff has increased as well.

The National Council on the Aging study (Leanse and Wagener, 1975) found that senior centers had few paid staff: one-third reported no full-time paid staff, 30 percent one staff member, 20 percent two or three, and 15 percent four or more. Twenty percent of multipurpose senior centers, and 50 percent of other centers reported no full-time paid staff. Surprisingly, data from the author's study conducted in the mid–1980s does not show much change in this variable. Table 3.4 shows that the number of senior centers reporting full-time paid staff were: 27 percent no staff, 25 percent one staff member, 21 percent two or three, and 26 percent 4 or more. The mean number of staff was three, and the median 1.4. Thus, the major change from the early 1970s was the greater likelihood of larger staffs.

The author's research also found a wide distribution in the number of part-time paid staff (Krout, 1987). As shown in Table 3.4, the mean number of part-time paid staff was 4.2, and the median 2.8. Earlier work by the author provides additional insight into paid staffing patterns (Krout, 1983). Not surprisingly, senior centers have a larger number of on-line paid staff than administrative staff, but the former are more likely to work part-time and to be over sixty (by a factor of two to one). The author's research also reveals the very large degree to which senior centers rely on volunteer workers, who overwhelmingly work part-time. Data in Table 3.4 show that two-thirds of the senior centers report no

Table 3.4
Number of Full- and Part-Time Paid and Volunteer Staff

Staff	Percent*
Number of Full-Time Paid Staff	
0	27.0
1	25.0
2,3	21.0
4,5	14.0
6 or more	12.0
Mean	3.0
Median	1.4
Number of Full-Time Volunteer Staff	
0	66.0
1	8.0
2	10.0
3 or more	17.0
Mean	2.6
Median	0.3
Number of Part-Time Paid Staff	
0	16.0
1	16.0
2	15.0
3	13.0
4,5	12.0
6 or more	28.0
Mean	4.2
Median	2.8
Number of Part-Time Volunteer Staff	
0	11.0
1-5	22.0
6-10	16.0
11-20	18.0
21-50	13.0
51 or more	20.0
Mean	40.7
Median	11.6

*N = 246
Source: J. Krout, (1987). Senior center linkages and the provision
of services to the elderly. Final report to the AARP Andrus
Foundation. Fredonia, New York.

full-time volunteer staff, with a mean and median of 2.6 and 0.3 respectively. Over one-half of the centers report more than 10 part-time volunteer staff, and 20 percent indicate over 50. The mean and median figures here are 41 and 12 (Krout, 1987). The author's earlier research again found differences according to community size. For almost every staff category reported—a notable exception being paid nutrition staff—rural senior centers report significantly smaller numbers. The total full- and part-time staff size is two and one-half times larger in central city than in rural centers, while the figure for volunteers is four and one-half times larger (Krout, 1983).

However, the number of senior center staff is only one of several indicators of personnel resources. One of the most important factors is the background of the senior center administrator or director. Given the growth of senior centers in terms of resources and activities, and the increasing educational expectations of society in general, one could expect to see changes in the demographics of senior center directors. Yet one might also expect these changes to be somewhat muted by the fairly heavy reliance on volunteer staff. The empirical evidence suggests a change towards greater professionalism (at least as indicated by level of education), but also clearly shows the wide variation in center administrator background.

The NCOA study (Leanse and Wagener, 1975) found the following educational levels for senior center directors: 7 percent, less than high school; 16 percent, high school graduate; 22 percent, some college; 26 percent, college graduate; and 16 percent, some graduate school. This study also reported that the director's level of education was positively related to the center's contacts with other aging organizations and the participation of center users in community affairs. However, this pattern may reflect the fact that better-educated directors tend to work in larger, more urban senior centers, and may not be a direct consequence of formal educational attainment. Data from the mid–1980s, shown in Table 3.5, reveal a considerable increase—almost a doubling—in the percentage of senior center administrators with more than a college education (Krout, 1987). Educational attainment was also found to be significantly higher for urban and suburban center directors.

The NCOA study also reported data on senior center director salaries; and these 1970s figures are quite low. The median was $9,000, and only 26 percent received a salary of over $10,000, while 2 percent earned $20,000 or more (Leanse and Wagener, 1975). By the mid–1980s, these numbers had changed considerably. The author found that slightly less than 25 percent of the directors worked as volunteers or earned less than $8,000; another 25 percent made from $8,000 to $15,000; 20 percent from $15,000 to $20,000; 21 percent from $20,000 to $29,999; and 6 percent were paid $30,000 or more (Krout, 1987). But as with other aspects of senior centers, these figures are influenced by the makeup of the sample used in the study. The salary distribution for center directors in the author's other national study was considerably lower, with only 30 percent as opposed to 48 percent of the directors reporting salaries of $15,000 and over

(Krout, 1983). But this sample was more rural than the first, and rural senior center directors tend to report considerably lower salary figures (Krout, 1983, 1987). Overall, salary figures also reflect the fact that some directors do not work full-time. Nonetheless, it would appear that senior center directors are not paid a salary commensurate with their expertise, experience, or responsibilities: as of 1987, less than 30 percent make more than $20,000.

Other center director characteristics, shown in Table 3.5, are also noteworthy. For example, almost 80 percent of directors are female, a fact that might partially account for, but not justify, the salary structure noted above. The median and mean age for center directors is fifty-two. Over 20 percent of the directors are aged sixty-five plus, and another 21 percent are between fifty-six and sixty-four; only 17 percent are thirty-five years or younger. Perhaps this should be expected, given the target population of senior centers. It may also reflect the fact that younger persons with similar educations can make more money in other occupations. Given this age distribution, it is not surprising to see a bimodal distribution in terms of years on the job: slightly over 40 percent of the directors report working in their position either three or less or six or more years.

SENIOR CENTER LINKAGES

Another organizational facet that will be discussed throughout this book is the linkage of senior centers with other agencies, organizations, and even individuals. Such linkages or working relationships expand the nature and scope of services senior centers provide for their participants (Krout, 1986b, 1987). Linkages take many forms, including referrals, use of other agency staff, exchange of information, or coordination of planning of services, to name but a few (Krout, 1986b, 1987). Since the extent and nature of these linkages are examined in great detail in chapter seven, no detailed discussion will be presented here. However, it is important to recognize that senior centers do maintain working relationships with a fairly large number and range of other entities in the communities, especially in regard to referrals. In fact, studies by the author have found that senior centers send referrals to an average of ten organizations (Krout, 1986b, 1987). Interestingly, most linkage arrangements are informal—they do not involve contracts or memos of agreement—but last several years. They involve Area Agencies on Aging and recreation and parks departments as well as hospitals, doctors, and religious organizations. For most types of services, more than 50 percent of the centers report working with other organizations, with sharing of information, referrals, and provision of staff being the most common types of assistance (Krout, 1987).

RESEARCH QUESTIONS

Information on the types of facilities and resources that characterize senior centers is extremely useful. It also has largely been ignored by most geronto-

Table 3.5

Background Characteristics of Senior Center Administrators

Characteristic	Percent*
Sex	
Male	21.6
Female	78.4
Years in School	
8 or less	1.8
9-11	3.1
12	20.8
13-15	24.0
16	19.9
17 or more	30.5
Degree	
None	3.5
High school/equivalency	35.7
Associates	9.1
Bachelors	30.4
Masters	19.1
Ph.D.	2.2
Number of Years in Position	
1	15.0
2	16.0
3	13.0
4	7.0
5	7.0
6-10	25.0
More than 10	17.0
Annual Salary	
Volunteer	12.0
Less than $4,999	6.0
$5,000 - 7,999	8.1
$8,000 - 11,999	11.5
$12,000 - 14,999	14.5
$15,000 - 19,999	20.1
$20,000 - 29,999	21.4
$30,000 or more	6.4
Age	
Up to 35	17.1
36-45	19.3
46-55	21.1
56-65	20.6
65 and over	21.9
Mean	52.0
Median	52.5

*N = 246

Source: J. Krout (1987). Senior center linkages and the provision of
services to the elderly. Final report to the AARP Andrus
Foundation. Fredonia, New York.

logical researchers. The cause and consequence of organizational linkages, budgets, staffing patterns, and facility characteristics as they relate to senior center operation, effectiveness or impact have not been studied. Researchers have paid little attention to senior center leadership, either by members or directors. Many of the volunteers in senior centers are also senior center participants (Krout, 1988), yet this type of volunteerism has received little empirical investigation. The development and day-to-day workings of senior centers have likewise attracted little notice from researchers.

Senior center directors report a wide range of goals. What influences these goals, and what determines the different emphases found among senior center directors? To what degree are center programming or state and federal funding congruent with these goals? Are the goals reflective of participant desires, or are they shaped more by center directors or boards of directors? While variation in the organizational identity of senior centers has been noted, virtually no data exist measuring the impact of organizational identity on goals, programming, participation patterns, participant characteristics, satisfaction with activities or center operation.

Similar questions can be asked in regard to facility characteristics and resources (budget and staff). Gerontologists have focused considerable attention on the impact of the built environment on the frail elderly, who either reside in the community or in long-term care facilities. Because senior centers are seen as the domain of the "well" elderly, little attention has been paid to the effect of these same variables on center activity or participants. The aging in-place of center users, along with the growing need for physical space for services such as adult daycare, suggests a need for more attention to this area.

The impact of center resources, especially through the number and charcteristics of staff, seems to provide particularly fertile areas for future research. It is assumed that centers with larger budgets and more staff offer a greater number and variety of programs. But how important are these factors? Are they related to participant satisfaction? Is a bigger center better or worse than a smaller one? Do significant variations exist between centers of similar physical and financial charcteristics? It has also been observed that over the years senior center budgets and staffs have increased, and that center directors appear to have become professionalized to some extent. What impact, if any, has this transition had on senior centers and their users? What caused it? Has the influx of federal program dollars "bureaucratized" senior centers, just as some have charged it has changed the nature and quality of the United States health care system? Does the receipt of Title III monies through Area Agencies on Aging reduce the flexibility of some senior center programming? Will senior centers become less dependent on federal dollars in the future? How would such a change affect their identity and operation?

These questions are, of course, related to other issues examined in this book. Unfortunately, since little is known about senior center organizational characteristics beyond the level of general description, discussion of them in later chapters will be limited. But, those who study senior centers should be aware of the impact of these characteristics. The bulk of senior center research has focused on center users as individuals, without consideration of how senior center goals, budgets, facilities and staff affect these users. This situation calls for a significant expansion in the scope of senior center research.

CHAPTER SUMMARY

This chapter has presented information on the organizational characteristics of senior centers in the United States, including goals, organization type, facilities, budget size and sources, staffing patterns and director characteristics, and linkages with other organizations. Considerable variation in all these factors exists among senior centers; there appears to have been some significant change over time in some of them (namely facilities, budgets). Major goals of senior centers, as noted in a survey of directors, include providing services, maintaining the independence of the elderly, and improving their quality of life.

As of 1987, three-quarters of the senior centers in this country are identified as multipurpose, a considerable increase over the 29 percent of the early 1970s. Two-thirds of the senior centers in this nation are subunits of other organizations, especially Area Agencies on Aging. The type and size of facility has been identified as vital to senior center operation and effectiveness. Since the early 1970s, the proportion of centers located in separate facilities has doubled, and the amount of space has also increased considerably. The budgets of senior centers have also grown: whereas the average senior center budget was $50,000 in the mid–1970s, it more than doubled, to $121,000, in the mid–1980s. While the availability of federal monies through the Older Americans Act has been an important impetus to senior center growth and diversification, centers actually depend on a wide variety of nonfederal funding streams.

Despite these increases in resources, centers still depend largely on volunteer labor. One-half of the senior centers in this country still report one or no full-time paid staff persons, and two or less part-time paid staff persons. There is evidence, however, to support the conclusion that senior center staff, at least center directors, have become more professional in terms of education, and presumably in work skills and performance as well.

The varied senior center characteristics examined in this chapter are often identified in the literature as important factors affecting the quantity, quality, and effectiveness of senior center activities. Yet empirical data on the relationship between these two sets of variables are strikingly absent from the literature. Indeed, this chapter has identified a large number of questions regarding organizational characteristics in need of further research.

REFERENCES

Cohen, M. (1972). The multipurpose senior center. In Senior centers: A focal point for delivery of services to older people. Washington, DC: National Council on the Aging.

Gelfand, D. (1984). *The aging network: Programs and services.* New York: Springer Publishing Company.

Kim, P. (1981). The low income rural elderly: Under served victims of public inequity. In P. Kim and C. Wilson (Eds.), *Toward mental health of the rural elderly.* Washington, DC: University Press of America.

Krout, J. (1983). The organization, operation, and programming of senior centers: A national survey. Final report to the AARP Andrus Foundation. Fredonia, New York.

Krout. J. (1984). The organizational characteristics of senior centers in America. *Journal of Applied Gerontology, 3,* 192–205.

Krout, J. (1986a). *The aged in rural America.* Westport, CT: Greenwood Press.

Krout, J. (1986b). Senior center linkages in the community. *The Gerontologist, 26,* 510–515.

Krout, J. (1987). Senior center linkages and the provision of services to the elderly. Final report to the AARP Andrus Foundation. Fredonia, New York.

Krout, J. (1988). The frequency, duration, stability, and discontinuation of senior center participation: Causes and consequences. Final report to the AARP Andrus Foundation. Fredonia, New York.

Leanse, J., and Wagener, L. (1975). Senior centers: A report of senior group programs in America. Washington, DC: National Council on the Aging.

Lowy, L. (1985). Multipurpose senior centers. In A. Monk (Ed.), *Handbook of gerontological services.* New York: Van Nostrand Reinhold Co.

Maxwell, J. (1962). Centers for older people: Guide for programs and facilities. Washington, DC: National Council on the Aging.

National Institute of Senior Centers (1978). Senior center standards, guidelines for practice. Washington, DC: National Council on the Aging.

4

Programming

INTRODUCTION

One of the criticisms levelled against senior centers is that their programming is too narrowly focused on social and recreational activities tailored to the needs, interests, and capabilities of "well" elderly in the working and middle classes. While such a view raises important issues, the author feels that senior centers provide a much broader range of programs that is generally recognized and serve a more varied population as well. Unfortunately, academic researchers and practitioners have not devoted sufficient energies to answer many of the important questions related to senior center programming.

This chapter identifies and examines these questions, beginning with a consideration of how senior center activities and services are conceptualized. The focus is, however, on contemporary programming. Specific attention is given to the numbers and types of center activities and services, the factors that account for their variation, the degree to which center programming meets the needs of "special" populations, the role that linkages with other organizations play in service offerings, and to participant satisfaction with center services and activities.

CONCEPTUALIZATIONS OF PROGRAMS

Before beginning this discussion, it is instructive to reflect on how senior center programs are classified. The word "program" is generally used to refer to the totality of activities and services offered by a senior center. Several attempts have been made to classify programs. Lowy (1985) places senior center offerings into four categories: direct services; services offered to and through other institutions; community action; and training, consultation, and research activity. Direct services include those types of programming generally associated with senior centers, such as recreation, education, social services, and nutrition services. Services offered to and through other institutions are provided to seniors off-site. Community action refers to service planning, coordination, and advocacy, while the fourth category is self-explanatory. This classification schema is somewhat unwieldy, because several of the categories are not mutually exclusive. The types of services included as "direct," for instance, may also be offered through other institutions or through community action.

The National Institute of Senior Centers classifies senior center services according to three categories, based on the recipient: individual services such as counseling, employment, and health maintenance; group services such as recreation, nutrition, education, and group social work; and community services or services provided by seniors to community institutions (Lowy, 1985). This schema has problems as well, for many types of services can be carried out in individual as well as group settings.

In addition, it has been suggested that services should be distinguished from activities (Krout, 1985). Activities are engaged in largely for personal enrichment or enjoyment. Services, on the other hand, are oriented more to meeting needs in specific areas such as health, nutrition, income, or in providing information about and access to the center. Services in this sense can be seen as more directly related to ameliorating or preventing problems, especially for at-risk seniors who may be frail, poor, or physically and socially isolated. Services are more likely to be means tested, but this practice is much less prevalent in senior centers than in traditional social service agencies.

The most common method of considering senior center programs is simply to break them down by the nature of the service or activity. The exact number of categories depends on how much detail a particular researcher cares to use. For example, as shown in Table 4.1, the National Council on Aging used twelve categories in its major report on senior centers and clubs in the early 1970s. More recent work by the author breaks senior center services into seven major categories (access to center, health and nutrition, in-home, income supplement, information and assistance, personal counseling, and special services), with thirty-eight subcategories, and senior center activities into four major categories (education, leadership opportunity, recreation, volunteer), with seventeen subcategories (Krout, 1985, 1987a). Cohen (1972), on the other hand, identifies thirteen such categories.

PROGRAMMING EXPANSION

It is clear that the breadth and depth of senior center programming has expanded considerably since the early days. While some pioneering senior centers, such as Little House, developed a wide range of offerings almost from the beginning, many others provided largely recreational and educational activities. But as senior centers enlarged their resource and user base, and as provisions of the Older

Table 4.1
Senior Center Activities

	Percent Offering
Active recreation (hiking, dancing, sports, exercise)	55
Creative activities (arts and crafts, drama, music, preparing bulletin/ newsletter)	86
Sedentary recreation (cards, bingo, movies, spectator sports, parties)	87
Nutrition (classes for counseling)	50
Classes, lectures, discussion groups	63
Counseling	55
Information and referral	69
Services (employment, health, legal, library)	51
Home-delivered meals	30
Meals on premises	54
Membership-governing groups (committees, board)	64
Leadership development training	23

Source: Leanse, J. and Wagener, L. (1975). Senior centers: A report of senior group programs in America. Washington: The National Council on the Aging, p. 29. Reprinted by permission from the National Council on the Aging, Inc.

Americans Act evolved to specify more clearly the types of services fundable at the local level, a progressive increase in service offerings followed. Some of the impetus for a greater number of diversity of programs no doubt came from seniors themselves as well.

The NCOA study (Leanse and Wagener, 1975) found the following breakdown for the number and types of services offered by senior centers in the early 1970s: 42 percent provided less than three services; 5 percent provided three basic services (education, recreation, information and referral or counseling); 31 percent reported the three basic services plus volunteer opportunities; and 22 percent provided the three basic services plus volunteer opportunities and health services.

Multipurpose centers naturally were much more likely to provide a wider range of services, with only 16 percent offering less than three services. These centers also were open for a greater average number of sessions (defined as morning, afternoon, or evening) than regular senior centers.

As shown in Table 4.1, the NCOA study found the following activities offered by the largest percentage of centers: sedentary recreation (87 percent); creative activities (86 percent), information and referral (69 percent); membership-governing groups (64 percent); and classes and lectures (63 percent). Meals on the premises had the largest average number of participants, followed by information and referral and sedentary recreation. Senior centers were also found to offer a large number of health services, ranging from direct provision of medical services to health education and counseling and transportation to treatment facilities. In addition, 60 percent of the centers reported having outreach programs. Finally, two-thirds of the centers indicated that their activities were directed at target populations, most frequently those persons age 60 or older and living in a fixed geographic area (Leanse and Wagener, 1975).

More detailed information on senior center activities and services in the 1980s has been collected and analyzed by the author (Krout, 1985, 1987b). This information was gathered as part of the project conducted in 1982–83, and involved a national random sample of 755 centers. Since this study is the most comprehensive and detailed available on senior center programming, considerable space will be devoted to a presentation of its findings. A technical discussion of the survey sampling and data collection procedures can be found in Krout (1983).

This study collected information on a large number of activities and services via a mail survey. Center directors were asked to indicate the availability of services in seven major categories: access; health and nutrition; in-home; income supplement; special services; information and assistance; and personal counseling and mental health services. Four activity categories were utilized: education, leadership opportunity, recreation, and volunteer. A total of thirty-eight services and seventeen activites were identified in this research. Data on availability of activities and services in general were analyzed by computing the number offered under the major headings.

These findings, presented in Table 4.2, show that two-thirds of the centers offer all of the activities identified under recreation and volunteer, while 42 percent offer no leadership opportunities. Over three-fifths of the centers offer five or more of the eight education activities. Data on services indicate that almost one-half of the centers offer no special or personal counseling services. However, almost three-quarters offer all three of the access to center services, and 43 percent provide all the health and nutrition services. Almost all of the centers offer at least one service in these categories. Considerable variation in availability was found for the in-home, income supplement, and information and assistance categories. Approximately one-quarter of the centers reported no in-home services, while close to 40 percent reported no income supplement services. Nearly 60 percent of the centers offer five or more of the eight information and

Table 4.2
Activities and Services Provided by Senior Centers for Major Categories

Category	Number of Services*									mean
	0	1	2	3	4	5	6	7	8	
Services										
Access to Center	6.6	7.7	13.9	71.8						2.5
Health and Nutrition	5.7	4.0	8.7	12.7	15.6	43.3				3.8
In-Home	23.6	14.0	14.7	14.6	10.9	7.0	15.2			2.8
Income Supplement	38.8	22.8	15.9	9.9	5.7	2.0	2.0	2.9		1.9
Special Services	48.9	21.1	12.1	7.2	7.2	3.7				1.1
Information and Assistance	13.0	4.8	7.5	8.6	8.5	11.7	9.9	13.2	22.8	4.7
Personal Counseling	46.4	15.2	13.1	9.3	16.0					1.3
Activities										
Education	4.6	4.8	8.2	8.2	11.9	15.1	18.1	12.5	16.6	5.0
Leadership Opportunity	42.1	16.4	16.0	25.4						1.2
Recreation	5.2	3.6	9.4	14.0	67.8					3.4
Volunteer	11.9	19.5	68.2							1.6

*Percentages based on N of 755.

Source: J. Krout. (1985). Senior center activities and services: Findings from a national survey. Research on Aging, 7, 3, 455–471. Reprinted by permission of Sage Publications, Inc.

assistance services. Thus, access to center, health and nutrition, and information and assistance are services most likely to be offered by senior centers (Krout, 1985).

The mean number of activities and services offered by centers is 11.1 and 17.6 respectively. Only 14 percent of the centers offer five or less activities; 18 percent provide six to nine; 23 percent offer ten to twelve; 20 percent provide thirteen to fourteen; and 25 percent make fifteen to seventeen activities available. Nine percent of the centers offer zero to five services; 12 percent provide six to ten services; 19 percent offer eleven to fifteen services; 22 percent provide sixteen to twenty services; 17 percent offer twenty-one to twenty-five services; 10 percent have twenty-six to thirty services; and 9 percent provide thirty-one to thirty-eight services.

Much more information on senior center activities and services can be gained from examining how often individual activities and services are offered. Data in Table 4.3 reveal considerable variation in this regard. For example, all but two educational activities, creative writing and library, are offered by a majority of the centers, but all of the leadership activities are offered by only a minority of the centers. Each of the recreation and volunteer activities is offered by at least 60 percent of the centers. Data in Table 4.3 also show variation in how often individual activities are offered. For example, leadership activities, parties, trips and educational activities are usually offered less than once a week. On the other hand, volunteer activities, active and sedentary recreation activities, arts and crafts and library activities are offered more frequently.

Data on the percentage of the sample that offers individual services and how often the services are offered are presented in Table 4.4. Almost all of the centers offer each access to center service—almost 90 percent offer information/referral, and 84 percent transportation. A large percentage of the sample also provides the health and nutrition services. Three-quarters of the surveyed centers offer health screening and maintenance, health education, and nutrition education, and almost nine in ten provide group meals. Two-thirds of the centers provide home-delivered meals. Most of the information and assistance services (consumer, housing, crime prevention, financial and taxes and legal aid, and social security) are offered by around two-thirds of the centers, while one-half of the sample reported providing information on welfare programs.

A smaller percentage of the centers reported in-home services. Three-fifths indicated providing telephone reassurance and friendly visiting, but only about 30 percent said they offer homemaker, home health, and home repair/winterization services. Special services, income supplement, and personal counseling and mental health services are generally offered by an even smaller percentage of centers—between 20 and 40 percent. Adult daycare is offered by just one in eight centers.

As was noted for activities, a large degree of variation was found in how often individual services are made available by centers. Some services, access to center and group or home-delivered meals, are offered more than three times

Table 4.3
Availability of Senior Center Activities

Activity	percent** offering	Availability*			
		less than once a month	1-3 times month	1-2 times a week	more than 3 times a week
Educational & Cultural					
Performing arts	52.7	38.4	28.1	24.6	8.8
Arts and crafts	87.0	4.3	11.6	38.7	45.5
Creative writing	26.1	54.8	12.2	28.4	4.6
Lectures	75.2	20.2	51.2	21.5	7.0
Library	49.3	23.7	20.2	10.8	45.4
Newsletter	66.0	27.7	67.1	3.0	2.2
Discussion groups	59.1	22.6	36.3	30.0	11.0
Trips	82.1	40.2	47.4	7.6	4.8
Leadership Opportunities					
Advocacy training	37.7	68.1	24.2	3.5	4.2
Participant government	40.7	45.6	46.3	3.6	4.6
Program leadership	46.4	34.3	36.3	11.1	18.3
Recreation					
Active	80.4	7.2	12.4	33.3	47.1
Sedentary	91.0	2.0	12.8	21.3	63.9
Parties	82.8	25.1	61.8	6.7	6.4
Trips	61.6	39.9	46.4	6.8	6.8
Volunteer Organization					
In center	86.8	2.9	5.2	6.7	85.2
In community	69.9	17.8	24.1	13.8	44.3

*Percentages only for those centers offering activity.
**Based on N=755.

Source: J. Krout (1985). Senior center activities and services: Findings from a national survey. Research on Aging, 7, 3, 455-471. Reprinted by permission of Sage Publications, Inc.

a week by a large percentage of centers. Others, such as information and assistance services and some health and nutrition services, are offered only once a month or less. On the other hand, in-home services, except home repair/winterization, are generally offered at least once a week.

Overall then, what do these data indicate? The 755 senior centers studied in this project provide an average of 11.1 activities and 17.6 services. But, as one might expect, the data also reveal considerable variation in the total number, type, and frequency of activities and services. Some types of activities and services are offered by a majority of centers: access to center, health and nutrition, information and assistance, recreation, and volunteer. On the other hand, a

Table 4.4
Availability of Senior Center Services

Service	percent** offering	less than once a month	Availability* 1-3 times a month	1-2 times a week	more than 3 times a week
Access to Center					
Information/referral	88.2	2.0	3.8	4.8	89.5
Outreach	78.4	4.6	12.5	12.2	70.8
Transportation	84.2	2.0	2.5	6.9	88.5
Health and Nutrition					
Screening & maintenance	75.4	17.0	46.5	15.1	21.4
Health education	76.7	20.6	46.1	17.3	16.1
Nutrition education	72.1	22.8	47.6	13.4	16.2
Group meals	87.8	1.2	5.1	5.9	87.8
Home delivered meals	66.4	4.8	1.8	6.0	87.4
In-Home					
Escort	43.8	12.4	13.6	17.2	56.8
Friendly visiting	57.2	8.8	22.9	17.4	50.9
Homemaker	32.6	13.8	8.5	16.3	61.4
Home health	29.7	20.1	17.4	12.5	50.0
Repair/winterization	34.7	42.4	12.6	8.8	36.3
Telephone reassurance	59.1	6.5	7.2	12.6	73.8
Income Supplement					
Crafts shop	38.4	27.9	6.6	9.0	56.6
Discount program	30.6	14.3	10.8	7.8	67.1
Food coop	11.4	33.7	23.3	20.9	22.1
Small appliance repair	9.9	50.7	14.7	12.0	22.7
Thrift shop	16.3	39.0	4.9	5.7	50.4
Job training	16.3	33.3	10.6	3.3	52.8
Job placement	26.5	35.0	12.5	5.5	47.0
Special Services					
Adult daycare	12.1	27.5	4.4	4.4	63.7
Crisis & emergency	29.5	30.5	15.7	7.2	46.6
Programs (handicapped)	24.1	25.8	14.3	12.1	47.8
Protective services	20.7	40.4	19.2	3.8	36.5
Nursing home programs	27.4	34.3	25.6	14.5	25.6
Information & Assistance					
Consumer information	67.8	29.7	26.2	7.4	36.7
Crime prevention	61.3	67.6	19.7	1.7	11.0
Financial/taxes	66.9	53.7	21.2	7.5	17.6
Housing information	63.4	37.0	18.4	7.3	37.4
Legal aid	66.9	41.4	33.5	7.7	17.4
Public assistance	35.5	35.1	21.3	6.7	36.9
Programs (SSI, etc.)	50.3	34.7	23.9	8.7	32.6
Social security/medicare	60.3	35.4	25.7	9.9	29.0

Table 4.4 (continued)

Service	percent** offering	less than once a month	Availability* 1-3 times a month	1-2 times a week	more than 3 times a week
Personal					
Crisis intervention	31.1	40.0	16.6	8.5	34.9
Group counseling	29.4	37.4	23.9	15.8	23.0
Individual counseling	47.9	20.4	16.3	17.7	45.6
Peer counseling	24.9	27.1	20.7	17.0	35.1

*Percentages figured only for those centers offering service.
**Based on N=755.

Source: J. Krout (1985). Senior center activities and services:
Findings from a national survey. Research on Aging, 7, 3, 455–
471. Reprinted by permission of Sage Publications, Inc.

number of other activities and services are generally not made available by senior centers: leadership, special services. Special, personal, income supplement, and in-home services are offered by the smallest percentage of the senior centers.

A comparison of these findings with data from the NCOA study reviewed earlier leads to the conclusion that the number and variety of senior center offerings grew considerably between the early 1970s and 1980s. In particular, it would appear that there has been a large increase in the percentage of centers offering home-delivered and group meals, information and referral, classes and lectures, and active recreation services (Krout, 1985).

Despite these findings, relatively little empirical research is available on senior center activities and services, and even less attention has been paid to changes in their availability over time. It seems likely that the program increases are partly a consequence of the increased federal commitment over the years to services that found a home in senior centers, such as supportive and nutrition services. Direct appropriations for senior centers grew as the Older Americans Act evolved during the 1970s; monies under Title III for center alteration and renovation, and even for staff support, increased considerably during this decade as well (Estes, 1980). State and local governments have also increased their interest in and funding of senior centers.

In addition, the targeting of senior centers in the 1978 amendments to the Older Americans Act as focal points for the provision of comprehensive community services to the elderly no doubt led to increased efforts at the local level to enlarge their offerings. The growing interest in the development of a continuum of care and service planning and coordination reflected in aging legislation of the 1970s also led to more visibility for senior centers, now viewed as vehicles to help overcome the problem of service fragmentation (Estes, 1980). Finally, the growth of senior center programming has likely been both a cause and consequence of their continued popularity with significant numbers of the elderly (Krout, 1985).

Why are some activities and services likely to be offered more frequently than others? One factor is the nature of the service. For example, centers do not normally offer parties, trips, or certain kinds of health or information services several times a week. The demand for such activities and services would not likely require or justify devoting resources to them so frequently. Differences in availability of activities and services also reflect varying levels of funding, and varying personnel and service costs. The author's research, however, did not determine the relative importance of each of these particular factors as predictors of activity and service availability, or the degree to which center offerings match service needs.

FACTORS ASSOCIATED WITH PROGRAMMING

The previous section presented data on the number and types of activities and services offered by senior centers. This section discusses what is known about the factors related to the variation in the quantity of senior center offerings. Again, several studies have examined this issue with national samples of senior centers.

The NCOA study found that senior centers designated as multipurpose offered more services than other centers. Over three-quarters of the multipurpose senior centers, but less than one-half of ordinary senior centers, offered four or more services (Leanse and Wagener, 1975). This study also reported that senior centers offering larger numbers of services had a larger number of participants and sessions, were located in more densely populated areas, and had better paid directors. However, the NCOA analysis was not detailed, was not based on a random sample, and did not employ any multivariate statistics.

The author's study, on the other hand, did use a national random sample, as well as multivariate analysis (Krout, 1987a, 1987b). The data reviewed in the previous section showed a large degree of variation in the number of services provided by a national sample of 755 senior centers. This variation can be further analyzed through multiple regression techniques. Multiple regression analysis allows for a determination of the relative strength of independent variables in explaining the variation in the data. The author's study provided information on three types of independent variables—characteristics of center users (percent female, nonwhite, aged seventy-five and over, and income less than $5,000), center organization and resources (budget, volunteer and paid staff, average daily attendance, center size, and multisite status), characteristics of the community where the centers are located (geographic region, community size, and percent of population aged 60 and over). The analysis revealed that these independent variables accounted for 25 percent and 21 percent of the variation in the number of activities and services, respectively. None of the community characteristics (except community type) and all but two of the center characteristics (average daily attendance and square feet in center) were found to be significantly related to this number.

Not surprisingly, the analysis showed that senior centers with larger budgets, more staff, and an affiliation with a multisite organization offered more activities and services. Several of the user characteristics were also found to have a significant impact on center offerings: senior centers with higher percentages of users who were aged seventy-five and over, nonwhite, and had incomes greater than $5,000 offered more activities. These findings indicate that the quantity of programming is related to the human and financial resources of a center, and participant characteristics, not its physical size or number of users. However, it should be noted that the strength of the relationship between these variables and the number of activity and service offerings can be characterized as modest at best, and that the proportion of variance explained by all the independent variables is not particularly strong.

A more recent study by the author (Krout, 1987a) revealed that senior center leadership may also be related to programming. In this 1986 study of senior center linkages, data were collected from a national sample of 246 senior centers. Activities and services were combined into a single dependent variable, and a multiple regression analysis was again performed to determine which variables are significantly related to the quantity of offerings. In addition to the independent variables used in the earlier survey, characteristics of the senior center director were also entered into the analysis (salary, sex, years on the job, age, education). Salary of the director was found to be positively related to, and the strongest predictor of, the number of activities and services offered by centers.

PROGRAMMING FOR SPECIAL NEEDS

One frequently heard criticism of senior centers is that their programming is overwhelmingly oriented to the healthy elderly, and that they do not try (nor are they well-suited) to serve the needs of more frail, isolated, and financially disadvantaged elderly. This criticism raises some fundamental questions about what senior centers can and should be expected to do, and about the role they should carry out in the network of support systems for the elderly. The validity and implications of this position will be discussed in several places in this book. This section looks at the more narrow issue of how prevalent special programming actually is in senior centers.

As is the case with many aspects of senior center operation, detailed data on special services are simply not as available as one would like. A number of authors have noted limitations in senior center programming as it relates to the needy elderly. For example, Hanssen et al. (1978) observe that senior center programming does not consistently address those elderly with physical limitations or mental health problems. As shall be seen in the next chapter, elderly who are frail physically and mentally, or are members of minority groups, make up a very small percentage of senior center users.

However, the author's research suggests that senior centers in general do offer some programming relevant to frail and at-risk elderly people. A 1982–83 research project (Krout, 1983, 1985) found that 12 percent of the 755 senior centers in the national sample offered adult daycare, 21 percent protective services, and 24 percent programs for the handicapped. Perhaps these figures should not be surprising, as the examination of senior center goals in chapter two revealed that meeting the needs of the frail or mentally and physically handicapped is not a high priority. A more recent study of senior center linkages revealed that more than half of the centers in the study reported few of these working relationships were directed towards the frail elderly, and three-quarters indicated few or some of their linkages were targeted towards minority elderly (Krout, 1987a). The latter finding probably reflects the relatively small number of center users who are minorities, and the small proportion of all senior centers nationwide that are located in minority neighborhoods or communities.

Unfortunately, very few studies of senior center services for specific types of special needs have been reported. One exception is a study on senior center programming for the hearing-impaired, carried out by Sela (1986). Of the almost 6,000 senior centers responding to an initial survey, only 9 percent reported having special programs and activities for this group, and 18 percent of these served hearing-impaired elderly only. Yet it is known that the prevalence of hearing loss rises significantly with age, and that slightly more than one-quarter of those aged sixty-five and over experience hearing loss (Ries, 1982). And, of course, some people are deaf or hard of hearing for all or most of their lives. In addition, various federal statutes have guaranteed equal access for the handicapped to all programs receiving federal dollars.

A recent survey of Maryland senior centers found that 45 percent reported serving the visually handicapped, one-third the hearing-impaired, and almost two-thirds the mobility-impaired (Maryland Association of Senior Centers, 1984). One of the more thorough considerations of the senior center role in serving frail or at-risk elderly was carried out by the National Institute of Senior Centers (Jacobs, 1980). A survey of a forty-four-state sample of 159 senior centers revealed that 84 percent of the sample reported attempts to serve at-risk elderly, despite severe funding limitations. And almost all of these centers coordinated their attempts with other community agencies. However, the representativeness of these findings must be questioned, as the response rate in the study was only 10 percent, and the sample most likely included senior centers more involved with programming for the frail elderly than generally is the case. In addition, the definition of at-risk used in the survey, the "frail, physically impaired and/or chronically ill" (Jacobs, 1980), is very broad and vague and creates difficulties in data interpretation.

Several more recent studies illustrate the difficulty of making generalizations about the degree of senior center involvement in programming for the frail elderly. Kendon et al. (1988) report that a recent national study of 1,200 adult daycare centers found that senior centers were the fourth most often cited referral source for freestanding adult daycare programs, and the second most frequently cited among non-freestanding programs as a sharer of space. On the other hand, Monk (1988) reports that directors of multipurpose senior centers in New York state indicated approximately 10 percent of their membership was frail, and that one-half felt they could not accommodate a larger percentage at their center. Four-fifths of the directors reported that they did not have programs for specific disabilities. Approximately one-half of the directors noted that the frail members participated in all or most of the center programming, while one-half indicated the frail were involved in only some of the programs. Finally, Short and Leon (1988) report that data from the 1987 National Medical Expenditure Survey reveal that only 7 percent of a sample of 7,000 functionally impaired elderly used a senior center.

There exists then, a conflicting and very limited amount of detailed information on the amount and nature of senior center programming for the frail or at-risk elderly. Yet, as senior center user populations age and become more frail, the need for such programming will increase signficantly.

PROGRAMMING LINKAGES

Although the extent and nature of linkages or working relationships that senior centers have with other organizations will be discussed in detail in chapter seven, their importance for center programming requires some attention here. The NCOA's landmark survey of senior centers and clubs paid some attention to these linkages (Leanse and Wagener, 1975), but the author's more recent studies (Krout, 1983, 1987a) examined this topic in much greater detail. Both of these studies generated large amounts of data from national senior center samples. One of the major conclusions supported by these studies is that senior center programming is significantly affected through the linkage process, in a number of ways. Perhaps one of the most important findings of this linkage research is that senior centers work with a wide range of organizations. These include local offices for the aging, social service agencies, recreation and parks departments, religious organizations, hospitals, health maintenance organizations, private physicians, chambers of commerce, schools, and libraries (Krout, 1983, 1987a).

The linkage data show that a majority of senior centers enlist the assistance of other organizations in the provision of their services. In doing so, they are able to make a wide range of services, or at least information about these services, available to their participants. The importance of linkages for center programming is considerable. Linkages increase the ability of senior centers to continue programming in the face of budget, facility, or personnel limitations. Linkages also constitute bridges between senior centers and other components of a service system that often appear to seniors as a bewildering array of disconnected programs. In this sense, they assist other organizations in carrying out their programming and goals. For many senior centers, linkage activity helps in the accomplishment of center goals and partly defines what senior centers are— linking organizations.

SATISFACTION WITH PROGRAMMING

Most students of senior centers assume that high levels of satisfaction with programs are the norm among senior center users. However, the author is not aware of any published studies that look closely at program satisfaction, or its correlates. The author's recently completed examination of participation patterns in eight senior centers found that 80 percent of the current users were very satisfied, and 17 percent somewhat satisfied with center activities (Krout, 1988). This, indeed, suggests a high level of satisfaction.

It is also interesting to note that in an earlier study (Krout, 1983), only 7 percent of a sample of center nonusers identified a dislike for the center of its participants as a reason for their lack of participation; only 10 percent of the center users who had decreased their frequency of attendance over time noted dissatisfaction with the center as a cause. However, in the author's recent study, 56 percent of the center users identified one or more problems at their centers. One-quarter noted only one problem, 14 percent noted two, and 16 percent felt three or more problems existed at their center (Krout, 1988). The percentage of the sample noting individual problems was as follows: lack of parking (21 percent); lack of air conditioning (15 percent); not enough space (14 percent); not enough transportation (12 percent); arguing among users (8 percent); and theft/stealing (7 percent). It is clear that the concerns are not directed to programming issues, but reveal some dissatisfaction with aspects of the physical center environment and of the behavior of fellow center users.

RESEARCH QUESTIONS

It is fortunate that gerontological observers have paid a fair amount of attention to the nature and extent of senior center programming in America. Nonetheless, some basic questions on this topic remain unresolved, and provide fertile ground for future investigations. One of the most basic has to do with how senior center programming can or should be conceptualized. Past research has tended to group all center programming together without consideration of its type, recipient characteristics, or objectives. Program typologies could aid in the understanding of what senior centers do and how they do it.

Some work has been carried out on the quantity of center programs, yet little is known about the degree of variation in programming, or the factors that account for it. The author's work has shown a moderate relationship between center resources (budget and staff size) and the number of senior center offerings, but these findings only scratch the surface of this topic. Much more needs to be learned about how and why some senior centers develop a large number and range of programs, and others do not. The author suspects that resources are only a part of the answer. What role do factors such as leadership, politics, and goals play in the growth and development of senior center programs? Indeed, the capabilities, interests, and motivations of center leadership (directors and advisory boards) are often identified by aging network professionals as key ingredients in programming successes and failures. Empirical data on this issue, though, are woefully lacking. In addition, this question is generally looked at from the resource or supply side, and not the demand side.

The existing information on senior center programming is limited in other respects as well. Basically, data are available on how many programs senior centers offer, but little is known about the nature of those programs. Without this information, it is difficult to address questions involving the impact and quality of senior center programming. Researchers simply are not in a position to provide carefully crafted empirical answers to the question of how well senior center resources are used and how they might possibly be used better. Again, it is clear that the variation in the content as well as the quantity of senior center programs is not currently well understood.

Other pieces of the programming puzzle are also missing. For example, senior center programming involves, and partly depends on, the expertise and skills of others obtained through the linkage process. But little information is available on the factors that account for this process. Again, this question will be considered in detail in chapter seven. It would appear that policy makers assume that the more services provided by senior centers, and the more linkages, the better. But is this necessarily the case? Should senior centers strive to do as much as they do, or are some of these programming efforts duplicating others? Are certain programs for the elderly more efficiently and effectively provided through other mechanisms or organizations? What problems arise through senior center programming not only for participants but for the aging services network in general? How can they best be resolvled?

Finally, the extent and success of senior center programming in meeting the needs of special populations—frail, disabled, low-income, minority—is simply not known. Some research suggests that senior centers may be doing an adequate job of meeting the needs of the frail elderly, while other findings do not support such a conclusion. Yet before senior centers are criticized for not doing enough in this area, it should be recognized that for many years senior centers were intended to provide for the well elderly almost exclusively. Can or should senior centers now be expected to incorporate large numbers of special need populations into their programming, especially in the absence of additional resources? If this is a reasonable and appropriate expectation, how do senior centers move toward such a goal?

CHAPTER SUMMARY

This chapter has presented an overview of senior center programming and programming issues. It is clear that the nature and extent of senior programming has grown considerably since the 1970s, and that senior centers in America today offer a wide range of activities and services to their participants. Indeed, data from a recent national survey of senior centers indicated that senior centers offer an average of eighteen services and eleven activities. These include access, health and nutrition, in-home services, counseling, information and referral, education, leadership, volunteer opportunities, and recreation. Senior centers with more financial, physicial, and personnel resources offer more of these services. Nonetheless, knowledge of the content of these programs and the factors involved in their development and operation is limited, and few studies have examined the factors responsible for the large degree of variation in programming.

The large majority of senior center programs are geared to the well elderly, and the ability and appropriateness of centers to expand efforts to meet the needs of special populations is not clear. While it would appear that senior center programs are well-received by their participants, research on how such programming can be improved is sparse. In many respects, the success or failure of center programming efforts has drawn little attention from gerontological researchers. Not only is research lacking on issues such as variation in content and quality, the conceptual basis for framing the necessary research questions is underdeveloped as well.

REFERENCES

Cohen, M. (1972). The multipurpose senior center. In *Senior centers: A focal point for delivery of services to older people*. Washington, DC: National Council on the Aging.

Estes, C. (1980). *The aging enterprise*. San Francisco: Jossey-Bass Publishers.

Hanssen, A., Meima, N., Buckspan, L., Henderson, B., Helbig, T., & Zarit, S. (1978). Correlates of senior center participation. *The Gerontologist, 18*, 193–199.

Jacobs, B. (1980). Senior centers and the at-risk older person. Washington, DC: National Council on the Aging.

Kendon, J., Hughes, S., Campione, P., & Goldberg, R. (1988). Shedding new light on adult day care. *Perspective on Aging*, November/December, 18–21.

Krout, J. (1983). The organization, operation, and programming of senior centers: A national survey. Final report to the AARP Andrus Foundation. Fredonia, New York.

Krout, J. (1985). Senior center activities and services: Findings from a national survey. *Research on Aging, 7*, 455–471.

Krout, J. (1987a). Senior center linkages and the provision of services to the elderly. Final report to the AARP Andrus Foundation. Fredonia, New York.

Krout, J. (1987b). Rural versus urban differences in senior center activities and services. *The Gerontologist, 27*, 92–97.

Krout, J. (1988). The frequency, duration, stability, and discontinuation of senior center participation: Causes and consequences. Final report to the AARP Andrus Foundation. Fredonia, New York.

Leanse, J., & Wagner, S. (1975). Senior centers: Report of senior group programs in America. Washington, DC: National Council on the Aging.

Lowy, L. (1985). Multipurpose senior centers: In A. Monk (Ed.), *Handbook of geron-tological services*. New York: Van Nostrand Reinhold Co.

Maryland Association of Senior Centers (1984). Report on MASC survey of senior centers. Unpublished report.

Monk, A. (1988). The integration of frail elderly into senior centers. Final report to the AARP Andrus Foundation. Columbia University, New York.

Ries, I. (1982). Hearing ability of persons by sociodemographic and health characteristics: United States: National Center for Health Statistics. *Vital Health Studies,* series 10, No. 140. DHHS Pub. No. (PNS) 82–1568, Public Health Services, Washington, DC: U.S. Government Printing Office.

Sela, I. (1986). A study of programs and services for the hearing impaired elderly in senior centers and clubs in the U.S. Unpublished dissertation. Washington, DC: Gallaudet College.

Short, P., & Leon, J. (1988). National estimates of the use of formal home and community services by the functionally impaired elderly. Paper presented at the annual conference of the Gerontological Society of America, San Francisco.

5

Awareness, Attitudes, and Utilization

INTRODUCTION

This chapter presents information on patterns of senior center awareness, attitudes toward senior centers, and overall center utilization rates among the elderly, as well as a general profile of center users. The focus is not only on whether or not seniors are aware that centers exist, but on how much they know about them and how they get this information. An investigation of the usage of senior centers begins in this chapter with a discussion of how many elderly attend senior centers, the activities they participate in, and a brief look at the socio-demographic characteristics of center users. A much more detailed examination of who uses senior centers and why, as well as the variation in attendance patterns, is found in chapter six.

As will be seen, the large majority of elderly in America are aware of senior centers, but do not have a very good understanding of what goes on in such places. That is, awareness or recognition does not necessarily equal knowledge. Only a modest percentage of the elderly in this country actually attend a senior center, but senior centers nonetheless are the most frequently used on any of the community services for the elderly. Yet among researchers, the understanding of what the elderly know about senior centers and how they and other age groups perceive such organizations is quite limited. This is unfortunate given the important role senior centers have come to play in the community-based support network of the elderly.

AWARENESS AND KNOWLEDGE

Although only a handful of studies have been done on the elderly population's awareness of senior centers, it would appear accurate to state that the large majority of the elderly are aware of these organizations. For example, Downing (1957) reported finding that two-thirds of a sample of sixty and over residents in Syracuse, New York had heard of a senior center or club. The author's own research of service awareness in western New York revealed that two-thirds of a sample of nonmetropolitan elderly had "heard of" senior centers (Krout, 1981), and that almost 80 percent of another sample of nonmetropolitan and metropolitan elderly were aware of "hot luncheon sites," all of which were housed in senior centers (Krout, 1984a). Another study of elderly in a small urban community found that all of the respondents, including those who did not use the senior center, were aware of a local senior center, and that 99 percent were able to identify correctly its location (Krout, 1982, 1984b). This is, of course, a very high degree of service awareness for an elderly population, and is probably due to the following factors: the community in which the study was conducted was small (15,000); the average number of years lived in the community for the sample was fifty-eight; the senior center had been in operation for fifteen years prior to the study; the center was physically very visible, and was housed in a separate structure only five years old (Krout, 1982, 1984b).

These are local studies; there is a paucity of data at the national level on senior center awareness. The major exception is the NCOA senior center and club study carried out in the early 1970s (Leanse and Wagener, 1975). These researchers found that two-thirds of a sample of senior center nonusers selected from a number of communities across the country had heard about the senior center in their area and, further, that three-quarters of these could describe its location correctly. One should not be completely dismayed by this lack of a current overall national figure for senior center awareness, since local variation is likely to be high.

The NCOA finding that three-quarters of the center nonusers knew the location of their local senior center illustrates a significant limitation of the data available on the awareness of senior centers. Researchers have generally asked elderly respondents if they have "heard of" senior centers, and have not actually measured knowledge of specific center programs or activities. Thus, the data can only be interpreted as showing that many elderly are aware that senior centers exist, not as indicating knowledge of what actually goes on in such places (Krout, 1983a). One of the few attempts to probe more deeply into the elderly's knowledge of services (not senior centers) speaks to this point. Snider (1980a) reports that for 75 percent of the health and social programs a sample of elderly Canadians was aware of, not even one specific service provided by that program could be identified. This finding underscores the need to distinguish between general familiarity with a program and specific knowledge of what it is or does.

The author has tried to probe the issue of awareness among the elderly of what senior centers actually do in a single-community study referred to earlier (Krout, 1982, 1984b). This project compared senior center and community service awareness, knowledge, and utilization patterns for a random sample of 125 elderly senior center participants versus 125 elderly nonparticipants. While all

Table 5.1
Activity and Service Awareness for Participants and Nonparticipants

Activity	Total Sample (n=250)	Percent Aware Participants	Nonparticipants
Center Activities			
Dinner parties	43	62	31
Cards	37	59	24
Square dances	35	56	23
Bingo	33	58	17
Trips	31	36	29
Senior club	30	60	10
Billiards	24	43	11
Exercise	22	47	7
Senior club	19	40	7
Crafts	19	38	7
Bowling	4	27	5
Sewing	8	19	3
Library	5	10	1
Golf	4	6	2
Community Services			
Luncheon program	84	98	76
Transportation	22	41	9
Information/referral	20	36	9
Meals on Wheels	14	22	9
Homemaker	7	9	6
Nursing	6	7	5

Source: J. Krout. (1984). Knowledge of senior center activities among the elderly. *Journal* of *Applied* *Gerontology*, *3*, 1, 71–81. Reprinted by permission of Sage Publications, Inc.

of the respondents said they were aware of the local senior center, the picture of their awareness changed quite drastically when they were asked to identify the specific activities and services available at or through the center. This is illustrated in Table 5.1, which shows the percentage of elderly senior center attenders and nonattenders who identified individual center activities and community services.

Not surprisingly, senior center participants were much more likely to be aware of activities and services than nonparticipants. Half of the senior center activities, and five of the six community services, were mentioned by less than 10 percent of nonparticipants. While the rates were much higher for center participants, the most well-known activity for them had a recognition rate of 62 percent. About one-half of the activities were not known to more than half of the participants. The most well-known center activity was noted by only 30 percent of the nonusers. These findings would suggest that those elderly who do not attend senior centers know very little about center programming. Even those who do attend have a selective knowledge of center activities, probably reflecting their personal interest in a relatively small number of activities.

These findings may well be subject to different interpretations. One interpretation is that senior center nonusers have little knowledge of center activities because they have little need of or interest in what goes on at such places. However, there are data suggesting that a significant minority of center nonusers might be interested in attending a senior center, and that a lack of awareness or understanding of what senior centers do may stand as an important roadblock to acting on this interest.

In addition, these findings suggest that senior centers, as is the case for many services for the elderly, do not do an adequate job of getting the word out to nonusers. Such a failure could be particularly problematic as senior centers are often viewed (as well as officially designated by Area Agencies on Aging) as focal points for the delivery of services to the elderly. But it should be noted that educating the public about senior centers, or about anything for that matter, is a substantial and complicated task. Some senior centers no doubt do a much better job of getting information out, and have more resources to do so, than others. And while it would appear that senior centers need to pay more attention to this issue, the fact remains that senior centers have a very high recognition factor among the elderly in general.

CORRELATES AND SOURCES OF AWARENESS

Before moving on to an examination of center utilization and users, it is instructive to consider two more aspects of senior center awareness: correlates and sources of awareness. Since those elderly who are not aware of or who know little about senior centers are unlikely to use them, information on the characteristics of those who are likely or unlikely to have such knowledge is important. Gerontologists have conducted some research to determine who among the elderly are more or less likely to be aware of services and senior centers, but the findings are mixed at best. The author's work on the nonmetropolitan elderly has shown that those elderly who were better educated, female, and married were aware of more social service programs than their counterparts (Krout, 1981). Snider (1980a, 1980b), on the other hand, found that the awareness of health and social services was not strongly associated with sociodemographic factors. Education, prior health service use, and monthly income were the strongest predictors of awareness in this study. The author has further found that the correlates of awareness vary for different types of services (Krout, 1985).

Unfortunately, very few studies have focused on senior center awareness. Ralston's (1985) study of the users of fifteen senior centers in Iowa found that knowledge of the number of center activities was greater for females, more frequent attenders, and for those with a more positive attitude toward the physical environment of the center. The author's study of senior center awareness found different correlates of awareness among center users and nonusers. While senior center participation was by far the strongest predictor of knowledge overall, the only variables associated with the number of senior center activities nonparticipants could identify was length of residence in the community, and whether or not an individual belonged to a senior club. Among participants, females and those with higher incomes knew of more activities (Krout, 1984b).

The other issue that has received scant attention from researchers is the source of information about senior centers. Many senior centers rely on newsletters or announcements in local newspapers to inform elderly in the community about what is going on at their centers. But there is little hard data to show one way or the other how effective these methods are in reaching the elderly. Gerontologists have found that informal networks play an important role in determining what the elderly know about services in general, as well as the likelihood that such services are used (Ward et al., 1984). It has been argued that "weak" informal ties (friends and neighbors) provide links to other networks, such as services, while "strong" ties (kinship) may hinder the spread of services knowledge to the elderly (Granovetter, 1973). Silverstein (1984) found that elderly who received information from both the media and informal sources had greater overall knowledge of services.

The author's study found considerable differences between participants and nonparticipants as to sources of information. The senior center newsletter was cited by the largest percentage of participants (42 percent) as a source of information on center activities, followed by the newspaper (21 percent) and friends or neighbors (19 percent). Virtually none of the nonparticipants cited the center newsletter, while 46 percent noted the newspaper and 41 percent friends or neighbors. Relatives, the radio, and other social organizations apparently played no role in providing information (Krout, 1984b). While limited in generalizability because they are from a small, one community sample, these findings suggest that senior center newsletters are not important conduits of center information for nonusers.

A final issue that should be considered is what the elderly think about senior centers—their attitudes or perceptions. Very little work has been done in this area, and the research on the elderly's attitudes towards services in general is somewhat ambiguous. For example, Kutner et al. (1956) found two-thirds of a sample favorably disposed to use an elderly medical center, while Schneider et al. (1985) report that two-thirds of a rural elderly Arkansas sample did not see senior citizen nutrition programs as a form of charity. Yet Powers and Bultena (1974) discovered that while their sample of elderly felt programs were important for the community, they were not appropriate for themselves. Powers and Bultena (1974) also report that the use of senior center programs was associated with a definition of the self as old that many elderly persons wished to avoid. These findings are echoed by Moen (1978), who writes of a "non-acceptor" syndrome among the elderly, in which a striving for independence is associated with a reluctance to admit needs or accept help, and even a denial of the use of services. Observers often point out that the elderly want to remain independent and self-reliant as long as possible (Coward, 1979).

One would expect those who attend senior centers to have a positive view of these organizations, but what about the elderly in general? There is no data to show that significant numbers of the elderly see senior centers in a negative light—as a form of welfare or charity. Studies of the factors related to center utilization have not found negative perceptions to be an important reason for nonattendance (Harris & Associates, 1975; Krout, 1983b). One study conducted by the author found that 100 percent of a sample of users, and 88 percent of a sample of nonusers, agreed or strongly agreed that "senior centers are a good idea." Center participants, however, were twice as likely to strongly agree with that statement. Slightly more than one-half of the nonparticipants, and three-quarters of the participants, agreed that revenues raised from taxes should be used to support the operation of senior centers (Krout, 1982). Thus, it would appear that the elderly do not generally view senior centers in a negative way, but (as will be demonstrated in the next chapter) this acceptance of the senior center "idea" does not translate into personal interest for many older Americans.

UTILIZATION RATES

It is difficult to say with certainty just what percentage of the elderly actually use senior centers, how frequent and intense this use is, and what activities and services the elderly participate in when they do attend. One finds considerable variation in the data on these questions, not only because of the different methodologies and research designs used by investigators, but also because senior centers themselves and the populations they serve are quite variable.

For example, data from a national study conducted in the early 1970s found that 19 percent of the elderly aged sixty-five to sixty-nine and seventy to seventy-nine, and 16 percent of those eighty and over, reported attending a senior center in the past year or so (Harris & Associates, 1975). A 1984 national study focusing on health and social situations of the elderly found that 15 percent had attended a senior center, and 8 percent had eaten a meal there, in the preceding year (National Center for Health Statistics, 1986). Local studies have reported a wide range of utilization rates. Scott (1983) found that 21 percent of an older rural Texas sample used senior centers, while the author found a utilization rate of 8 percent for a rural New York sample (Krout, 1981). Thus, it would appear reasonable to state that between 10 to 20 percent of the elderly in this country attend senior centers at least once a year. However, it should be noted that these studies may actually undercount the degree of senior center utilization, since they focus on current or relatively recent use. It is quite likely that the percentage of seniors who have ever attended a senior center is higher.

The 10 to 20 percent figure translates into from 2.6 to 5.3 million people aged sixty-five and over. This figure should probably be increased by around one or one and one-half million, to include an additional ten or more percent of the almost eleven million persons aged sixty to sixty-four. The total number of senior center users, then, might well be as high as seven million, and could even be higher if one considers that at least some nonusers might want to participate but do not for one reason or another. For example, Harris & Associates (1975) found that 21 percent of center nonusers fit into this category. While this number is impressive, some no doubt would argue that it is conservative, and that ten million users is a more correct figure (Pothier, 1985). It is difficult to reconcile different estimates, because data on center use is not collected consistently or in a uniform manner. A five to seven million figure refers to unduplicated users, and higher numbers might include some duplicate counts.

However, there are indications that the utilization rate of senior centers for the elderly, especially those in their sixties has recently declined. While no hard data are currently available on this issue, information collected as part of a national study of Area Agencies on Aging conducted by the author seem to indicate this trend (Krout, 1989). The majority of the over one hundred rural AAA directors interviewed in this study have reported significant declines in senior center attendance in their planning and service areas.

Almost every director has indicated that these declines result from an aging in place of participants who have attended centers since the 1970s. As these people age, they become less healthy and can no longer come to the center. Some become in-home service clients, some move in with family or go into nursing homes, and some die. This aging cohort of senior center users is not being replaced by the "young-old." The AAA directors indicate that many senior centers do not offer activities that are of interest to a healthier, wealthier, and more mobile group of recent retirees. These elderly are not comfortable with the idea of going to a "senior" center. Whether or not senior centers can successfully adjust to this trend may well be one of the most important issues facing senior centers today. It should be noted, however, that many senior centers are not experiencing this participation decline.

Besides knowing how many elderly attend senior centers, it is also instructive to know what they do there. This information also provides some insight into the reasons for and the impact of senior center participation. Senior centers report offering a wide range of health, social, and educational activities. But just because centers make these programs available does not mean all center users are involved with them.

Unfortunately, gerontological researchers have paid little attention to rates of participation in particular senior center activities. Leanse and Wagener (1975) did query a national sample of center users about this, and uncovered the following participation rates: table games, 70 percent; tours and trips, 63 percent; meals, 49 percent; creative, 46 percent; educational, 36 percent; governance, 31 percent; special services, 25 percent; information/referral and outreach, 12 percent; and leadership, 6 percent. Data on participation in activities by the users of eight senior centers studied by the author show a somewhat different pattern (Krout, 1988). Since all but one of the centers served as a nutrition site, it is not surprising to find that over 80 percent of the participants reported eating a noon meal at the center. One-half reported attending dinner or birthday parties, while about 40 percent participated in volunteer activities, trips, bingo, and cards or board games. Slightly more than one-quarter engaged in the exercise programs. Close to 20 percent took part in arts and crafts, reading, dances, music-related activities, and center business or board meetings. Only 14 percent played pool, probably because only a few centers had pool tables and because pool is considered a male activity. Participants were involved in an average of five different activities.

PARTICIPANT CHARACTERISTICS

The final issue examined in this chapter is who senior center participants are. As usual, generalizations are risky, because most senior centers draw their users from a fairly limited geographic area, and have user populations that reflect those areas. Centers located in minority communities will have largely minority users, while those in more affluent largely white suburbs will have white, middle-income users. Data collected in the NCOA study (Leanse and Wagener, 1975) reveal the following participant profile: 50 percent were aged sixty-five to seventy-four, while less than 5 percent were aged eighty-five or over; 82 percent were white, 10 percent black, and 8 percent other; three-quarters were female; six of ten lived alone; and 10 percent were physically disabled.

A more recent national survey conducted by the author on a smaller sample of senior centers found the following averages for participant characteristics: 18 percent under sixty-five, 53 percent between the ages of fifty-six and seventy-four, and 30 percent aged seventy-five and over; 73 percent female; 65 percent unmarried; and 82 percent white (Krout, 1987). Comparisons between these two studies should be made with great care, but may indicate two things. Senior center participants are probably older today, and the racial breakdown has not changed over time. Indeed, as has been suggested, the client base of many senior centers may well be becoming older as participants age and as fewer people in their sixties find senior centers attractive.

The characteristics of senior center users reported in other studies show both similarities and dissimilarities to these national profiles. For example, a sample of center participants studied by the author in the early 1980s (Krout, 1983b) was three-quarters female, had an average age of 71.5, and was relatively healthy. In addition, 42 percent lived alone, slightly less than half were married, the average number of years of education was less than ten, and only one in six had incomes over $10,000 a year.

A more recent study of eight senior centers found somewhat different participant characteristics (Krout, 1988). These characteristics are shown in Table 5.2. Slightly more than two-thirds were female, the median age was seventy-two,

Table 5.2
Socio-Demographic Characteristics of Senior Center Participants

Variable	Percent (N=235)
Sex	
Male	32.8
Female	67.2
Age	
Less than 60	6.0
60-64	10.3
65-69	17.6
70-74	27.0
75-79	20.6
80 or more	18.5
Median	72
Race	
White	83.8
Black	16.2
Marital Status	
Married	43.9
Widowed	47.8
Other	8.3
Living Situation*	
Live alone	50.4
Live with spouse	39.7
Live with child	12.1
Other	7.4
Education (years)	
8 or less	24.6
9-11	26.7
12	29.2
13 or more	19.5
Income (monthly household)	
Less than $500	29.6
$500 - $699	25.4
$700 - $999	20.2
$1,000 or more	25.0
Home Ownership	
Own	61.6
Rent	38.4

*Percents do not add up to 100 because some elderly live with a spouse and child.

Source: Krout (1988). The frequency, duration, stability, and discontinuation of senior center participation: Causes and consequences. Final report to the AARP Andrus Foundation. Fredonia, New York.

almost one in six was black, half lived alone, slightly more than half had monthly household incomes of less than $700, and three-fifths were homeowners. However, considerable differences were found between centers. For example, most of the blacks in this eight center sample attended one inner-city senior center, and the average age at another center was eighty-five.

Several researchers report users are physically and mentally well (Hanssen et al., 1978; Rosen et al., 1981; Tuckman, 1967) and largely blue-collar (Kent, 1978; Rosenzweig, 1975; Rosow, 1967; Tissue, 1971). By and large, there is little in these data to dispute Lowy's description of the average senior center user as a lower to middle-middle class white female in her late sixties or early seventies with low to middle income and some high school education. She is not functionally impaired, belongs to several clubs and is socially oriented having friends in and out of the center (Lowy, 1985).

It is important to note that, overall, minority elderly are underrepresented in senior centers, while white ethnics are probably overrepresented. Yet national data collected in the mid–1970s show that 40 percent of blacks aged fifty-five and over not participating in a senior center would like to attend one (Harris & Associates, 1975). Why don't blacks utilize senior centers? Ralston (1982) found lack of access (transportation), absence of culturally appropriate programming, and lack of need due to informal helping networks to be major obstacles to senior center participation among blacks. In another study, Ralston (1984) found that blacks were much more likely to want to attend senior centers if the activities they suggested were made available.

RESEARCH QUESTIONS

It is clear that researchers have only begun to scratch the surface of what the elderly know about senior centers, how they perceive them, and how many attend them. Much of what is known about these topics is based more on inference from studies of services in general, than on hard data from representative samples of different age groups. A 1986 National Center for Health Statistics study did look at utilization of services, including senior centers, in a cursory way, but did not query elderly respondents about their awareness or knowledge of centers. These are several issues and questions that should be included in a much-needed research agenda.

First, there simply is not enough information concerning how much the elderly (and other age groups) know about senior centers, and how they come to know it. It is important to distinguish between awareness that senior centers exist or that their focus is on older people, and actual knowledge or understanding of what senior centers do. Most elderly persons appear to recognize the term senior center, and to be aware that senior centers operate in their communities. But, beyond that general awareness, the large majority of elderly who do not attend senior centers know little about them.

Much more needs to be learned about the characteristics of center nonusers, with their varying degrees of knowledge about senior centers. Is the knowledge of center activities and operation up to date and accurate? Where does the information come from? These are important questions for those who want to increase awareness, and thereby center attendance, among elderly who might benefit from senior centers. To many people, older and younger, the terms senior "center" and senior "club" both have a largely social or recreational connotation. Questions of awareness and knowledge of senior centers are also relevant to policy issues surrounding changes in the role senior centers play, or could play, as a means of bringing services to an elderly population that has increasing numbers of both healthy and vulnerable individuals.

Equally important is the need for a better understanding of the perceptions the elderly and others have of senior centers. Awareness and attitudes are clearly related to the use of senior centers. But they also are important to the future of senior centers, especially in the area of resource allocation. As society increasingly scrutinizes the cost of health and social programs for the elderly, will it be as generous as it has been in the past in providing federal and local funds to senior centers? Existing evidence, although quite limited, suggests that senior centers are perceived positively, or at worst neutrally, by both elderly people and the public at large. Yet researchers have not investigated why this is so, or considered what might change these opinions. These questions ought not be viewed solely from the center survival point of view, but also from a broader policy perspective. Discussions of the roles that senior centers will be able to successfully play in coming years must consider the image they have presently and are likely to have in the future.

The utilization rate of senior centers is clearly a topic in need of more research. The current national figure is estimated to be 15 percent of the sixty-five and over population, but there is considerable local variation in this number. One of the most basic questions is why local usage rates vary. What roles do center resources and leadership, population demographics, accessibility factors, local culture and so on play in explaining different rates? Put another way, what kinds of centers have low or high utilization rates? It is also necessary to begin to pay serious attention to the changes in center usage rates, especially projections for future groups of the elderly who are now in their sixties, fifties or even early forties. What is likely to happen to utilization figures if the focus of senior centers begins to shift to a more service-oriented model for the frail or less physically mobile? Finally, the research in these areas must become more focused, and consider not just utilization in general, but utilization of specific senior center activities and services.

CHAPTER SUMMARY

This chapter has examined what the elderly know of and think about senior centers, and the overall utilization rates of these organizations by the community-dwelling elderly. The research indicates that almost all of the elderly in this country are aware of the senior centers that are located in their communities. And while most of the elderly have a vague idea of what senior centers are and do, nonattenders can only identify a small number of the programs actually found there. Overall, older people in this nation have a positive view of senior centers— even if they may not want to attend one.

While the actual number of senior center users among the sixty and over population varies from community to community, it would appear that a national estimate of 10 to 20 percent is an accurate figure. Regardless of the exact figure, senior centers are the most frequently used of any of the local aging network services. This fact reinforces the argument that a better understanding of senior center operation, utilization, and impact is needed.

Unfortunately, this chapter has also noted the relative lack of studies on awareness, attitudes, and utilization of senior centers. Several researchers have carried out examinations of the levels and correlates of center programming awareness, but most studies are restricted in terms of focus, sample size, and analysis. Longitudinal studies are virtually nonexistent, and the limited data base makes the projection of trends and the building of estimates most difficult. Relatively little is understood about how the elderly come to know about senior centers, and what shapes their (and other age groups') attitudes and perceptions of centers. This is not an encouraging state of affairs for researchers, policy makers, or practitioners; it needs to be improved if informed decisions are to be made about senior centers now and in the future.

REFERENCES

Coward, R. (1979). Planning community services for the rural elderly: Implications for research. *The Gerontologist, 19,* 175–282.

Downing, J. (1957). Factors affecting the selective use of a social club for the aged. *Journal of Gerontology, 12,* 81–89.

Granovetter, M. (1973). The strength of weak ties. *American Journal of Sociology, 78,* 1360–1380.

Hanssen, A., Meima, N., Buckspan, L., Henderson, B., Helbig, T., & Zarit, S. (1978). Correlates of senior center participation. *The Gerontologist, 18,* 193–199.

Harris, L., & Associates, Inc. (1975). *The myth and reality of aging in America.* Washington, DC: National Council on the Aging.

Kent, D. (1978). The why and how of senior centers. *Aging.* May-June, 2–6.

Krout, J. (1981). Service utilization patterns of the rural elderly. Final report to the Administration on Aging. Fredonia, New York.

Krout, J. (1982). Determinants of service use by the aged. Final report to the AARP Andrus Foundation. Fredonia, New York.

Krout, J. (1983a). Knowledge and use of services by the elderly: A critical review of the literature. *International Journal of Aging and Human Development, 17,* 9–23.

Krout, J. (1983b). Correlates of senior center utilization. *Research on Aging, 5,* 339–352.

Krout, J. (1984a). The utilization of formal and informal support by the aged: Rural versus urban differences. Final report to the AARP Andrus Foundation. Fredonia, New York.

Krout, J. (1984b). Knowledge of senior center activities among the elderly. *Journal of Applied Gerontology, 3*, 71–81.

Krout, J. (1985). Service awareness among the elderly. *Journal of Gerontological Social Work, 9*, 7–18.

Krout, J. (1987). Senior center linkages and the provision of services to the elderly. Final report to the AARP Andrus Foundation. Fredonia, New York.

Krout, J. (1988). The frequency, duration, stability, and discontinuation of senior center participation: Causes and consequences. Final report to the AARP Andrus Foundation. Fredonia, New York.

Krout, J. (1989). Area agencies on aging: Service planning and provision for the rural elderly. Final report to the Retirement Research Foundation. Fredonia, New York.

Kutner, B., Fanshel, D., Togo, A., & Langner, T. (1956). *Five hundred over sixty*. New York: Russell Sage.

Leanse, J., & Wagener, L. (1975). Senior centers: A report of senior group programs in America. Washington, DC: National Council on the Aging.

Lowy, L. (1985). Multipurpose senior centers. In A. Monk (Ed.), *Handbook of gerontological services*. New York: Van Nostrand Reinhold Co.

Moen, E. (1978). The reluctance of the elderly to accept help. *Social Problems, 25*, 293–303.

National Center for Health Statistics. Stone, R. (1986). Aging in the eighties, age 65 years and over—Use of community services; Preliminary data from the Supplement on Aging to the National Health Interview Survey: United States, January-June 1984. *Advance Data From Vital and Health Statistics*. No. 124, DHHS Pub. No. (PHS) 86–1250, September 30, Hyattsville, Maryland: Public Health Service.

Pothier, W. (1985). Senior centers: An update before it's too late. Unpublished manuscript.

Powers, E., & Bultena, G. (1974). Correspondence between anticipated and actual use of public services by the aged. *Social Services Review, 48* 245–254.

Ralston, P. (1982). Perception of senior centers by the black elderly: A comparative study. *Journal of Gerontological Social Work, 4*, 127–137.

Ralston, P. (1984). Senior center utilization by black elderly adults: Social, attitudinal and knowledge correlates. *Journal of Gerontology, 39*, 224–229.

Ralston, P. (1985). Determinants of senior center attendance. Paper presented at the Annual Meeting of the Gerontological Society of America, New Orleans.

Rosen, C., Vandenberg, R. J. & Rosen, S. (1981). The fate of senior center dropouts. In P. Kim & C. Wilson (Eds.), *Toward mental health of the rural elderly*. Washington, DC: University Press of America.

Rosenzweig, N. (1975). Some differences between elderly people who use community resources and those who do not. *Journal of the American Geriatrics Society, 23*, 224–233.

Rosow, I. (1967). *Social integration of the aged*. New York: Free Press.

Schneider, M., Chapman, D., & Voth, D. (1985). Senior center participation: A two-stage approach to impact evaluation. *The Gerontologist, 25*, 194–200.

Scott, J. (1983). Older rural adults: Perspectives on status and needs. Paper presented at the annual meeting of American Home Economics Association, Milwaukee.

Silverstein, N. (1984). Informing the elderly about public services: The relationship between sources of knowledge and service utilization. *The Gerontologist, 24,* 37–40.

Snider, E. (1980a). Factors influencing health service knowledge among the elderly. *Journal of Health and Social Behavior, 21,* 371–377.

Snider, E. (1980b). Awareness and use of health services by the elderly: A Canadian study. *Medical Care, 18,* 1177–1182.

Tissue, T. (1971). Social class and the senior citizen center. *The Gerontologist, 11,* 196–200.

Tuckman, J. (1967). Factors related to attendance in a center for older people. *Journal of American Geriatrics Society, 15,* 474–479.

Ward, R., Sherman, S., & LaGory, M. (1984). Informal networks and knowledge of services for older persons. *Journal of Gerontology, 31,* 216–223.

6

Participants and Participation

INTRODUCTION

The previous chapter discussed what is known about senior center awareness and overall utilization patterns. This chapter examines in detail the characteristics of the elderly who attend senior centers and the reasons for their participation in center activities. These topics have probably received more attention from academic researchers than any other facet of the senior center phenomenon, although it is evident that the findings are far from conclusive or exhaustive. A major emphasis will be on integrating the work that has been carried out over the years on comparisons of senior center users versus nonusers. In addition, research on the variation in utilization patterns is also explored, as is the topic of senior center "drop-outs."

A consideration of the factors related to senior center attendance and the variation in attendance patterns provides another piece in the puzzle of what senior centers are and the roles they play in the lives of elderly users and the community. Most of the research on these topics has focused on single sites or communities, but findings from several national samples of elderly are available. While inconsistent findings abound, some generalization is possible.

SOCIO-DEMOGRAPHIC, HEALTH, AND ACCESS FACTORS

Much of the research on senior center participation and participants has focused on comparing the characteristics of center users to those of nonusers. A much smaller number of studies has examined variation in utilization patterns for users. The amount of research on this topic precludes a detailed discussion of each study's findings. However, a close look at the types of variables used in this body of literature and a summary of what has been found will provide considerable insight into who uses senior centers and why. These variables can be broken down into several categories: socio-demographic; health and well-being; accessibility; and social contact. The small body of literature devoted to variation in attendance among users has also utilized these factors.

Socio-demographic factors include variables such as sex, age, race/ethnicity, marital status, and socioeconomic status. Women, for example, have been found to be disproportionately represented among senior center populations (Harris & Associates, 1975; Krout, 1983a). However, the role that gender plays as a differentiating factor between users and nonusers is not clear. Several studies report equal rates of senior center utilization for men and women (Hanssen et al., 1978; Silvey, 1962; Storey, 1962; Tuckman, 1967) and one study reports greater use among males (Schramm and Storey, 1961). A recent national study found that 12 percent of the males and 17 percent of the females aged sixty-five to seventy-four used a senior center in 1984 (National Center for Health Statistics, 1986).

The impact of age is equally ambiguous. Several studies of single centers using small samples (Hanssen et al., 1978; Krout, 1983b) have found no user versus nonuser age differences. However, national data for 1984 collected by the National Center for Health Statistics (Krout et al., 1989) reveal that the percentage of elderly using senior centers does increase with age, at least until age eighty-five. The percentage of individuals reporting they attended a center at least once in the previous year was 7 percent for those aged sixty to sixty-four, 13 percent for those aged sixty-five to sixty-nine, and 17 percent for those in their seventies and early eighties. The percentage dropped to 13 percent for those aged eighty-five and over. These data show that participation rates increase with age, but the reasons for this increase have not been empirically demonstrated. Declines in health, labor force participation, and income, loss of spouse and friends due to death, and fewer opportunities for independent travel are some of the changes that can accompany aging and may account for the observed age-related participation rates.

Others have reported that senior center users are overrepresented in the sixty-five and over category (Storey, 1962; Harris & Associates 1975). This should not be surprising, however, as senior centers evolved with the stated purpose of serving older Americans, and because funding regulations of many center programs often include age restrictions. The recent trend toward the decline in participation of the "young-old," and the aging in place of center participants noted by AAA directors and others, suggest that center users may well be older on average than nonusers (Krout, 1989).

It is generally argued that minority elderly are less likely to participate in senior centers because of the lack of center availability and accessibility in minority areas, ignorance or neglect of cultural considerations in center programming, and the presence of strong informal support systems in minority communities (Harris & Associates, 1975; Downing and Copeland, 1980). Race and ethnicity have received little attention from senior center researchers, and the few available studies have yielded mixed results. Several studies have found race does not differentiate between center users and nonusers (Demko, 1980; Hanssen et al., 1978; Silvey, 1962; Storey, 1962; Tuckman, 1967), while Harris & Associates (1975) reported blacks were somewhat more likely to have attended, and much more likely to want to attend, a senior center or club. Interestingly, Ralston's (1985) study of factors affecting the utilization of senior centers in a medium-sized Midwestern community found older blacks more likely than older whites to express an interest in attending a senior center, if the activities they suggested were offered. Finally, one of the few studies of senior center use among elderly blacks found no differences between attenders and nonattenders on age, marital status, and sex (Ralston, 1984a).

A number of studies also report no differences in marital status (Hanssen et al., 1978; Silvey, 1962; Storey, 1962; Tuckman, 1967). A study by the author (Krout, 1983b) did find that 48 percent of center users, versus 70 percent of the nonusers, were married and that users, not surprisingly, were therefore twice as likely to live alone. However, it should be noted that these differences were not significant when subjected to multivariate analysis. The National Center for Health Statistics data (1986) are very similar: they show that 20 percent of those aged sixty and over living alone or with a nonrelative attended a senior center, versus 11 percent of those who lived with a spouse or other relative.

Socioeconomic status is somewhat more complex and is usually broken down into three components: education, occupation, and income. Research indicates clearly that center users do not have higher educational levels than nonusers. It is less clear whether or not they have lower educational levels. While some studies have found such a difference (Krout, 1983b; Leanse and Wagener, 1975; Rosenzweig, 1975), others have not (Hanssen et al., 1978; Harris & Associates, 1975; Silvey, 1962; Storey, 1962; Tuckman, 1967). A similar situation is found for the relationship between occupation and senior center utilization. One study found center users more likely to have blue-collar occupations (Rosenzweig, 1975), several others reported no occupational differences (Hanssen et al., 1978; Silvey, 1962; Storey, 1962; Tuckman, 1967), and two revealed a greater representation of white-collar workers among center users (Tissue, 1971; Trela, 1976). As for income, several studies report users to have lower incomes than nonusers (Harris & Associates, 1975; Krout, 1983b), and the data from the National Center for Health Statistics (Krout et al., 1989) reveal that the percentage of elderly attending senior centers declines as income increases. While income differences might simply reflect education, occupation, and sex differences, the author's study found income to be a significant predictor of center utilization in a multivariate analysis that included these and other socio-demographic measures (Krout, 1983b).

As for health and well-being, several studies report that senior center users have fewer, or less serious, health problems than nonusers. These include examinations of national elderly populations (Leanse and Wagener, 1975) as well as local ones (Tissue, 1971; Tuckman, 1967). The National Center for Health Statistics data (Krout et al., 1989) reveal that larger percentages of elderly who view their health positively and report few daily living problems attend senior centers. Hanssen et al. (1978) and the author (Krout, 1983b), however, found similar health levels for senior center users versus nonusers.

The concept of well-being includes dimensions such as loneliness and life satisfaction. Senior centers have been viewed as well suited for warding off loneliness (Frankel, 1966; Maxwell, 1962), but this potential benefit of center participation has received little attention from researchers. One study reports senior center users were more lonely than nonusers (Hoppa and Roberts, 1974) while Leanse and Wagener (1975) found no difference in loneliness for these two groups. The findings on the relationship between center use and life satisfaction are more consistent, with users reporting higher levels of life satisfaction (Leanse and Wagener, 1975; Tissue, 1971) and less depression (Hanssen et al., 1978). However, Toseland and Sykes (1977) have questioned the causal nature of this relationship, and Ralston (1984a) suggests that senior centers are just one of many factors that may contribute to higher level of life satisfaction for senior center users.

The third factor receiving attention from researchers, accessibility, has been operationalized as distance lived from center, availability of transportation, and place of residence. Problems with accessibility are often given a high priority as reasons why the elderly do not use services. Several studies have found that center attenders live closer to senior centers than nonattenders (Leanse and Wagener, 1975; Tuckman, 1967) while Hanssen et al. (1978) report this not to be the case. Tuckman (1967) even found that distance was related to senior center use when awareness of the center was controlled. Yet research on the availability of transportation suggests that it may not play as an important role as a facilitator or inhibitor of center use as has been supposed. Leanse and Wagener (1975) did not find differences between users and nonusers in their perceptions of transportation as being a problem. Availability of transportation is not reported to differentiate users from nonusers by Hanssen et al. (1978). A comparison of users and nonusers of a senior center in a small city by the author revealed that car ownership, frequency of car use, and need for transportation were not significant predictors of center utilization (Krout, 1983b).

The third indicator of accessibility, place of residence, usually refers to the size of the community in which a person lives and is often classified as rural versus urban. One of the most consistent and strongest findings to emerge from studies of services for the elderly is that rural elderly populations have a smaller number and range of services available to them, and that these services are less accessible than in urban areas (Krout, 1986). Harris & Associates, (1975), for example, report that senior centers are less accessible to the rural than the urban elderly. It should be noted, however, that rural areas are not lacking for senior centers, and that the percentage of all senior centers in this country that are rural is probably somewhat greater than the percentage of the total elderly population that lives in rural areas. Rural centers are located in smaller facilities, have fewer resources, and report lower attendance figures (Krout, 1984, 1985). A recent study by Sela (1986) indicates that 32 percent of some 6,000 senior centers nationwide responding to a 1985 survey were in fact rural. The author found a similar figure in earlier research (Krout, 1983c).

The lower degree of availability and accessibility of rural services would suggest lower senior center utilization rates among the rural elderly. Several studies have found this to be the case for a wide range of services, including senior centers (Auerbach, 1976; Krout, 1983c; Osgood, 1977; Powers and Bultena, 1974). However, not all researchers report this relationship. May et al. (1976) uncovered no rural versus urban differences for participation in a nutrition program, and Taietz (1970) found considerably greater senior center attendance rates for the rural elderly. He reports that the percentage of elderly utilizing senior centers declined progressively from 26 percent for places of less than 2,500 to 4 percent for suburban and central city dwellers. However, more recent data from the National Center for Health Studies (Krout et al., 1989) do not reveal such a trend. Center utilization rates were somewhat larger for nonmetropolitan, nonfarm elderly (15 percent) than suburban (14 percent) or central city (12 percent) elderly, but fell off to 8 percent for farm dwellers. It should be kept in mind that in many small towns, the senior center may serve as the central, perhaps the only location where elders can receive certain services (Krout, 1986). Thus, the role senior centers play in the lives of the rural elderly may be greater than elsewhere because of the lack of other community-based alternatives.

SOCIAL CONTACT

Social contact, the last factor, has consistently been found to play an important role in senior center use, but the nature of this role is unclear. For example, some studies show that users have more contact with friends and family (Daum, 1982; Krout, 1983b; Ralston, 1984b; Tissue, 1971), while other researchers report that nonusers have greater contact (Rosenzweig, 1975). The author (Krout, 1983b) has argued that center users may have average levels of contact with family and friends, but find these inadequate for their needs and hence attend centers for additional social interaction. Some elderly may attend senior centers to make up for a lack of social contact in their lives, while others fulfill a high need for social activity through center participation.

But the complexity and importance of social contact may be missed by research that simply measures the amount of interaction with family or friends. Several researchers have focused on the role that senior center users play as confidants for one another (Leanse and Wagener, 1975; Ralston, 1985). The National Council on the Aging's study in the early 1970s found that one-half of the confidants of participants attended the same center (Leanse and Wagener, 1975). However, it may well be that this confidant relationship existed before and did

Table 6.1
Reasons for Attending Senior Centers

Reason	1st Ment (n=234)	2nd Ment (n=223)	Percent 3rd Ment (n=168)	4th Ment (n=95)	Most Important (n=222)
Activities					
Enjoy volunteering	6.0	3.1	2.4	5.3	7.7
Learn new things	—	—	—	2.1	0.5
Get out of house	6.0	3.1	5.4	8.4	4.1
Trips/specific activities	7.3	9.4	7.7	16.8	7.7
Keep busy	6.0	1.3	1.8	3.2	3.2
Fun place	4.7	4.0	4.8	3.2	2.3
Lots of information	—	—	1.2	—	—
Activities in general	8.1	14.8	18.5	8.4	13.5
Nothing better to do	2.5	0.9	1.8	—	0.5
TOTAL ACTIVITIES	40.6	36.6	43.6	47.4	39.5
Social Interaction/Companionship					
Enjoy the people	7.7	4.5	6.0	1.1	7.7
Fellowship	8.5	8.1	9.5	5.3	19.4
They care	—	0.4	—	1.1	—
Like the staff	3.8	0.9	3.0	3.2	0.9
Talk with others same age	11.1	4.5	6.5	2.1	6.8
Be a part	5.1	9.0	5.4	4.2	3.6
Friends/spouse go there	8.1	12.6	9.5	8.4	9.0
Meet people	0.9	2.2	0.6	3.2	0.5
TOTAL SOCIAL INTERACTION/ COMPANIONSHIP	45.2	42.2	40.5	28.6	47.9
Health & Nutrition					
Convenient	3.4	4.5	3.6	5.3	2.7
Good meals	8.1	11.7	5.4	6.3	6.3
Inexpensive meals	—	—	—	1.1	—
Health checks	—	—	—	1.1	—
Spouse/parent/self sick	—	—	0.6	—	—
Easier because of health	—	0.9	—	—	—
Keeps you healthy	—	—	—	—	—
Keeps you independent	—	—	—	—	—
TOTAL HEALTH & NUTRITION	11.5	17.1	9.6	13.8	9.0
Attitudes/Outlook					
To feel young	—	—	—	2.1	0.5
Feel good about self	—	—	—	2.1	0.5
Positive outlook on life	—	—	—	—	—
Get outside self	—	—	—	—	—
Something to look forward to	0.4	—	0.6	—	—
Feel useful	0.4	0.4	1.2	2.1	1.8
Keep mind active	—	—	—	—	—
Not to be alone	0.9	0.9	1.2	1.1	0.5
Need it	—	—	—	—	—

Table 6.1 (continued)

Reason	1st Ment (n=234)	2nd Ment (n=223)	Percent 3rd Ment (n=168)	4th Ment (n=95)	Most Important (n=222)
TOTAL ATTITUDES/OUTLOOK	1.7	1.3	3.0	7.4	3.3
Other					
More time	---	---	---	---	---
More money	---	---	---	---	---
It's inexpensive	---	0.9	1.8	---	---
Transportation	0.4	---	1.8	1.1	0.9
Other	0.4	1.8	---	2.1	---
More activities	---	---	---	---	---
TOTAL OTHER	0.8	2.7	3.6	3.2	0.9

Source: J. Krout (1988). The frequency, duration, stability and discontinuation of senior center participation: Causes and consequences. Final Report to the AARP Andrus Foundation. Fredonia, New York.

not result from senior center attendance. Other observers argue that people do not come to senior centers to establish new or replace old, primary relationships, but rather to further less personal, secondary relationships (Bley et al., 1972; Gelfand and Gelfand, 1982). It has also been noted that senior center users tend to be "joiners" (Freedman and Axelrod, 1952; Storey, 1962; Tuckman, 1967). Leanse and Wagener (1975) found that not only were senior center users more likely to belong to other social organizations at present, they were more likely to report having done so at age thirty-five.

The importance of social contact and relationships is reinforced by findings from the small number of studies where elderly were asked specifically why they got involved with senior centers. Over one-half of the center users interviewed as part of the NCOA study (Leanse and Wagener, 1975) said they joined to meet others, while one-half also said that opportunities for leisure time were important. The author's comparison of reasons for senior center use and nonuse found three main reasons for attendance: something to do (47 percent); invitation from friends (24 percent); and to be with people or make friends (17 percent) (Krout, 1983b). These findings are similar to those reported by Carp (1976) and Trela and Simmons (1971).

A more recent study of senior center participants and participation conducted by the author provides more detailed data on the reasons for participation (Krout, 1988). Data presented in Table 6.1 show responses from a sample of over 200 senior center users. Specific reasons are grouped into general categories for up to four responses, and the most important reason is shown as well. Responses indicating social interaction and companionship were given by the largest percentage of center participants, with activities a close second and health and nutrition a distant third. The most frequently identified ''most important'' reasons were: fellowship (19 percent); activities in general (14 percent); friends or spouses attend (9 percent); enjoy volunteering, trips and other specific activities, enjoy the people (eight percent each); talk with others the same age (seven percent); and good meals (six percent).

Some data on the reasons why the elderly do not attend senior centers is also available. The NCOA Study (Leanse and Wagener, 1975) found lack of knowledge of center location (29 percent), being too busy (23 percent), transportation problems (20 percent), and health problems (16 percent) to be the most frequently identified reasons for nonparticipation. Of these four reasons, only being too busy (38 percent) was also reported by Cryns (1980) in a study of elderly in a metropolitan suburb and the author (Krout, 1983b) in a small city study (40 percent). The elderly in both of these studies were most likely to indicate being too busy and not having any interest (29 and 19 percent) as reasons for nonparticipation. Other reasons were identified by only a small percentage of respondents. Lack of awareness of location or availability of centers were not noted by any of the elderly respondents in these two studies. It is interesting that the percentage of the samples indicating lack of transportation decreases, while the percentage indicating they did not feel old enough increases over time. And while it should be noted that this trend is based on comparing cross-sectional data, these findings suggest that reasons for lack of participation in senior centers have changed since the 1970s. The primary reasons today appear to be the active life styles of seniors, and lack of interest in senior center activities. This finding suggests that senior centers may have to change some of their activities if they are to attract more participants, and that a fairly large percentage of the elderly simply may be too involved in other things to have the time or interest to attend senior centers.

Of course, the reasons for nonparticipation can be hypothesized to vary for seniors depending on age, sex, race, and class. One of the few studies to examine reasons for nonparticipation according to race, sex, and socioeconomic variables found a significant difference by socioeconomic status for only one of five reasons, lack of interesting activities (Ralston and Griggs, 1985). No differences based on race or sex were found. However, the NCOA study (Leanse and Wagener, 1975) did reveal more differences: younger elderly were more likely to indicate that they did not feel old enough, while those over seventy-five were two and one-half times more likely to cite poor health as a reason for nonparticipation. Also, rural residents and minority elderly were much more likely to indicate lack of facilities as a reason.

VARIATION IN ATTENDANCE

It is evident from the previous section that considerable research has been carried out on senior center use, particularly in the form of comparisons of users versus nonusers. As the author has argued elsewhere (Krout, 1983b), the usefulness of research on senior center utilization is limited, due to the practice of conceptualizing and describing senior center attendance as an act rather than as a continuum ranging from nonuse all the way to former use. The vast majority of studies compare users versus nonusers without investigating the different levels of frequency, duration, and intensity of center participation. Ferraro and Cobb (1988) observe that this practice involves limitations that prohibit in-depth examinations of center participation. Thus, little is known about the dynamic nature or process of senior center involvement.

Yet study of the frequency, duration, and stability of senior center use has important conceptual, practical, and policy implications. Information on variation and change in center use can contribute to the building and assessment of participant and participation typologies. It can help researchers answer questions about the correlates of center involvement among users, the degree to which center users exhibit changes in levels of activity, and the accuracy of existing models of center use.

From a more practical perspective, an understanding of the variation in attendance level and length would surely be of value to practitioners. Knowledge of individual utilization would help center staff identify users—particularly those who are "needy"—who are likely to reduce or terminate their involvement. This information would also be useful in planning for the programming and staffing needs of senior centers. A center that can expect a relatively high involvement, low turnover population surely would have different needs than one that serves a population likely to be short-term, low involvement users.

A greater understanding of the variation in the frequency and duration of center involvement would also inform those involved in making policy decisions regarding the impact of senior centers of the elderly, and their role in the continuum of support for the elderly. Questions about the level and length of senior center involvement take on considerable importance when viewed in relation to changes that have occurred in the elderly population over the past several decades. For example, the average sixty-five-year-old in this country is somewhat healthier and wealthier, and will live significantly longer than his or her predecessors. The implications of this for senior center use patterns could be better understood if more data were available on the dynamics of attendance for current users.

Few empirical studies have evaluated the impact of senior centers on their users. Research that simply determines the number of center participants and user versus nonuser differences is not sufficient to make such judgements. The intensity and length of involvement is an important piece of the assessment puzzle. Finally, a broader conceptualization and measurement of senior center involvement is germane to an extremely important and basic issue—the targeting of resources to the low-income, frail, and minority elderly. Knowledge of the number and characteristics of elderly center users is not sufficient to determine the degree to which senior centers serve these groups.

The studies that have examined variation in senior center participation patterns have rarely presented descriptive statistics on this variation, but have instead focused on its correlates. Thus, little if anything is known about how frequently or how long center participants attend a center. The author has examined this issue in two different studies—one a single-center study (Krout, 1983b) and the other an eight-center study (Krout, 1988). Each of these studies collected data on the variation in the frequency, duration, and change in frequency of attendance among center participants. The biggest difference in the two studies is for frequency of attendance. In the more recent study, one-third of the participants attended every day, and one-half several times a week, while corresponding figures in the earlier study are 5 percent and 34 percent. No striking differences were found for duration of attendance. The participants in the eight-center study were more likely to have attended their centers for from one to three and ten years or more. About one-half of the participants in each study reported a stable frequency of attendance, while participants in the more recent study group were much more likely to show an increase (36 versus 21 percent) in how often they went to their center.

Several researchers have investigated the correlates of variation in frequency or regularity of attendance, and their work is of particular interest to the topic at hand (Demko, 1980; Ferraro and Cobb, 1988; Krout, 1983b, 1988; Ralston, 1985; Silvey, 1962; Tuckman, 1967). These studies have generally not found that socio-demographic variables such as sex, age, race, marital status, occupation, education, and income differentiate between low- and high-frequency users. However, others find frequency of attendance greater for those elders who live closer to senior centers (Ralston, 1985; Tuckman, 1967). Once again, the roles of social contact and health are not clear. Demko (1980) found that low-frequency users had more opportunities for alternative activities (belong to other clubs, live with others, and have more contact with family and friends), while Tuckman (1967) uncovered no relationship between these two variables. While Tuckman (1967) reports that more frequent attenders were in better health, Ferraro and Cobb (1988) found them to be in poorer health and to be more likely to eat a meal at the center. They conclude that more frequent attenders are more likely to score low on measures of morale. Bley et al. (1972) found "erratic" users much more likely to use the center as a social agency.

Several researchers have examined a second dimension of attendance, length or duration of use. Ralston (1985) reports that long time attenders were older, less educated, more likely to be female, and less likely to use a car to get to the center, and concludes these characteristics indicate higher levels of social need. Ferraro and Cobb (1988), on the other hand, found length of utilization greater for those who live with others and have higher levels of life satisfaction.

The author's two studies also examined the correlates of frequency and duration of senior center attendance through the use of multivariate statistics. Since somewhat different independent variables were used in each study, their comparability is limited. In one study, frequency of attendance was found to be greater for participants who were female, had less frequent contact with their children and more frequent contact with their friends, and higher levels of self-assessed health

(Krout, 1983b). In the other study, it was greater only for those attenders who lived closer to the center and had more frequent contact with friends (Krout, 1988). Duration of attendance was not statistically related to any of the variables in one study (Krout, 1988) and greater for those who were older and had higher levels of self-assessed health in the other (Krout, 1983b).

These studies also asked senior center participants the reasons for increased or decreased participation. For the single-center study, the most often noted reasons for increased frequency of attendance were enjoyment of activities (34 percent), availability of more activities (21 percent), and more free time and involvement with friends at the center (14 percent). One-half of the reasons given for decreased frequency of attendance related to a decline in health, while 20 percent indicated less free time due to other activities. Ten percent of the responses expressed dissatisfaction with center involvement (Krout, 1983b). These findings underscore the importance of health and social contact as reasons for changes in frequency of center participation.

The author's more recent study of the participants and participation patterns at eight senior centers in several rural and urban western New York communities collected detailed data on the reasons for changes in the frequency of attendance (Krout, 1988). Data on up to three reasons as well as the most important reasons for increased participation are presented in Table 6.2. Reasons concerning center activities were identified by the largest percentage of participants overall, followed by social interaction and companionship, "other," and health and nutrition. The specific first-mentioned reasons selected by the largest percentage of the participants were: activities in general (22 percent); more time (19 percent); enjoying volunteering (15 percent); more activities (11 percent); and friends or spouse go to the center (8 percent). However, this order changes for the most important reason: friends or spouse go to center (17 percent); activities in general (13 percent); enjoying volunteering (12 percent); and more time (10 percent). Reasons for a decline in participation are quite similar to those found in the author's earlier study (Krout, 1983b). A decline in health is noted by almost one-half of the participants, and another ten percent note a decline in their spouse's health as a most important reason. Ten percent also note being busier than before, and being employed, as reasons for decreased participation (Krout, 1988).

Perhaps the least studied aspect of senior center participation is the cessation of center involvement. An extensive review of thirty years of senior center research reveals that only three publications have addressed this issue. Perhaps the most comprehensive of the studies (Trela and Simmons, 1971) found that 20 percent of a suburban center's members stopped attending after one year, and one-half dropped out after two. One-third of the center users dropped out because they were too busy, while 15 percent noted health problems. Another 15 percent had died and another 12 percent were unhappy with the center or its activities.

In another study, Hanssen et al. (1978) found former senior center users

Table 6.2
Reasons for Increased Senior Center Participation

Reason	1st Ment (n=83)	Percent 2nd Ment (n=20)	3rd Ment (n=48)	Most Important (n=78)
Activities				
Enjoy volunteering	14.5	8.3	10.0	11.5
Learn new things	---	---	5.0	2.6
Get out of house	2.4	2.1	---	3.8
Trips/specific activities	1.2	8.3	---	3.8
Keep busy	2.4	2.1	---	1.3
Fun place	2.4	2.1	---	1.3
Lots of information	---	2.1	---	---
More activities	10.8	8.3	---	6.4
Habit	1.2	---	---	---
Activities in general	21.7	14.6	5.0	12.8
Nothing better to do	---	---	5.0	---
TOTAL ACTIVITIES	56.6	39.6	25.0	43.6
Social Interaction/Companionship				
Enjoy the people	2.4	---	5.0	2.6
Fellowship	1.2	---	15.0	5.1
Help care	---	---	---	---
Like the staff	---	4.2	---	---
Do/talk with others same age	---	---	5.0	1.3
Be a part	---	---	5.0	---
Friends/spouse go there	8.4	25.0	15.0	16.7
Meet people	---	---	---	---
TOTAL SOCIAL INTERACTION/COMPANIONSHIP	12.0	29.2	45.0	25.6
Health & Nutrition in General				
Convenient	2.4	---	---	2.6
Good meals	1.2	---	---	2.6
Inexpensive meals	---	---	---	---
Health checks	---	---	---	---
Spouse/parent/self sick	2.4	2.1	---	3.8
Easier because of health	2.4	4.2	---	2.6
Keeps you healthy	---	---	5.0	---
Keeps you independent	---	---	---	---
TOTAL HEALTH & NUTRITION	8.4	6.3	5.0	11.6

Table 6.2 (continued)

Reason	1st Ment	Percent 2nd Ment	3rd Ment	Most Important
	(n=83)	(n=20)	(n=48)	(n=78)
Other				
More time	18.8	8.3	10.0	10.3
More money	1.2	───	───	1.3
It's inexpensive	───	───	───	───
Transportation	3.6	2.1	10.0	6.4
Other	───	4.2	5.0	1.3
TOTAL OTHER	22.9	22.9	25.0	19.3

Source: J. Krout (1988). The frequency, duration, stability, and discontinuation of senior center participation: Causes and consequences. Final report to the AARP Andrus Foundation. Fredonia, New York.

reported less walking ability, more feelings of depression, and lower levels of social activity than current users. Finally, Rosen et al. (1981), in a comparison of senior center users who dropped out for health versus nonhealth related reasons, found the former to see their health as poorer, be more dependent on others for transportation and socialization, and be less optimistic about the future. They also compared drop-outs from rural and urban centers and found the rural drop-outs were poorer, less healthy and active, more socially isolated, more lonely and unhappy, and more likely to have transportation problems. In addition, few if any supportive services were available in rural areas for these drop-outs.

The author's recent study of variation in senior center participation considered cessation of attendance in detail (Krout, 1988). Working with sign-in sheets, the names of several hundred ex-participants were identified. The majority of these individuals could not be interviewed because they had moved away, died, entered a long-term care facility, or simply could not be located. However, seventy ex-participants were successfully interviewed and compared with current center attenders in the sample. One-half of the ex-attenders cited health problems as the most important reason for their withdrawal from senior center activities, 13 percent noted access problems and ten percent indicated they just wanted to stay home. Thus, three-quarters gave what could be interpreted as health, mobility, or activity reasons. Another 10 percent indicated a dislike for the center activities (especially food) or how the center was run, and 17 percent noted other things to do as the most important reason. These responses indicate that dissatisfaction with the center or other social involvements by themselves generally do not lead to withdrawal from a center.

However, the importance of each of these is actually greater as a contributing factor. One-third of the ex-attenders indicated two reasons for ending participation; and one-third of these expressed negative comments about the center and one-quarter noted other things to do. Another one-third also noted access problems. None of these individuals indicated health problems as a second reason. These data suggest that health problems predominate as the single most important cause, and are always chosen as such even when an individual notes more than one cause. But other problem areas, such as lack of access or dissatisfaction with the center, are also important. Alternative activities are relatively unimportant.

These data suggest that former senior center participants are worse off than current participants; data on socio-demographics and measures of health, life satisfaction, and social contact support this hypothesis. Former participants are much older, more likely to be widowed, less educated, and poorer than current participants. Data shown in Table 6.3 reveal that current center participants see their health and their lives much more positively than former participants. And while current users have much higher levels of contact with friends and neighbors, no significant differences are found on frequency of contact with children (Krout, 1988). It is difficult to determine the degree to which these characteristics are a cause or consequence of senior center withdrawal or indicate characteristics associated with a higher risk of withdrawal—part of a high-risk profile that could be used by center staff to identify potential drop-outs and thus to delay or prevent withdrawal.

The "chi square" numbers reported in Table 6.3 allow a determination of whether the relationship between user status and variables such as health is statistically significant. A significant relationship is one that is unlikely to have happened by chance. The greater the chi square number, the smaller this probability. A chi square that yields a probability of at least .05 is generally considered significant (the lower this figure, the greater the significance).

All of these studies are limited in their generalizability due to small sample sizes, but they do seem to indicate that former center users are less well off than current users. This underscores the importance of senior center participation for the elderly, as well as of learning more about the reasons for and consequences of withdrawal from center involvement.

IMPLICATIONS OF FINDINGS FOR MODELS

What can be concluded from these findings on senior center participants in terms of senior center user models? First, it is clear that no single profile fits all senior center users and, therefore, it is unlikely that any one model will predict who will use such centers and why they will use them. The divergent findings on the relationship between center attendance and socio-demographic, health and life satisfaction, accessibility, and even social contact variables indicate what is already known—there is great variation in senior centers and their user/nonuser populations. Thus, to make a general statement that the "voluntary action" as opposed to the "social agency" model (Taietz, 1976) should be used when conceptualizing senior center issues is probably not valid. The users of some

Table 6.3
Comparison of Current Versus Former Senior Center Participants on Selected
Variables

Variable	Former (n=70)	Current (n=235)	Chi Sq	sig
Present Health*				
Excellent	8.6	23.7		
Good	34.3	43.4		
Fair	34.3	28.1		
Poor	22.9	4.8	27.08	.000
Health Compared to Others*				
Better	20.0	57.5		
About the same	70.0	36.7		
Worse	10.0	5.9	10.41	.006
Overall Life Satisfaction*				
Very satisfied	31.4	63.2		
Somewhat satisfied	48.6	32.9		
Somewhat dissatisfied	14.3	3.9		
Very dissatisfied	5.7	---	22.61	.000
Frequency of Contact with Neighbors*				
Daily	14.7	53.9		
Several times a week	59.9	30.4		
Once a week	8.8	4.3		
Few times a month or less	20.5	11.3	36.86	.000
Frequency of Contact with Friends*				
Daily	2.9	24.5		
Several times a week	38.2	40.2		
Once a week	32.4	10.0		
Few times a month	11.8	17.9		
Once a month or less	14.7	7.4	29.83	.000
Frequency of Contact with Children				
Daily	17.2	22.6		
Several times a week	34.5	20.0		
Once a week	13.8	19.0		
Few times a month	20.7	15.9		
Once a month or less	13.8	22.6	7.57	.111

*Significant at the .05 level or better.

Source: J. Krout (1988). The frequency, duration, stability, and
        discontinuation of senior center participation: Causes and
        consequences. Final report to the AARP Andrus Foundation.
        Fredonia, New York.

senior centers are better educated, healthier, wealthier, and more likely to engage
in high levels of social activity than others. Since senior centers are often multipurpose, they may serve a more heterogeneous population than other social
organizations. This point leads to a second observation: gerontologists may well

need to develop better models or typologies to describe the empirical diversity of the senior center phenomenon.

With these first two observations standing as caveats, it certainly does appear that many senior center users are active and activity-seeking people who attend centers for the recreational, educational, and social opportunities offered there. Senior centers generally appear not to serve socially isolated or frail people to a great degree, but some centers do affect these populations. From this perspective, Taietz's (1976) voluntary action model is applicable. But attenders may also have needs—nutrition, health, and social—that are not met in other ways.

Many elderly persons enjoy activities and social contact but do not use senior centers. Why? Is it their attitude toward their own aging that leads them to see attendance at a senior center as a personal as well as public admittance of being old? Interestingly, some senior center users may well be more active and healthy, and may age much more successfully, precisely because of their center involvement. The role that senior centers play in preventing or postponing illness and isolation will be considered further in chapter eight.

RESEARCH QUESTIONS

This chapter has shown that while research findings are available, the understanding of senior center use and users remains incomplete. Studies have been conducted on the characteristics of the elderly who attend senior centers, but most of them are limited conceptually, methodologically, and by virtue of their often small and geographically restricted samples. The problem is not simply insufficient research, but a lack of research that focuses on the central questions of senior center utilization. These central questions are outlined below.

First, researchers should move away from the current, rather crude conceptualization of usage as a yes or no dichotomy to a more sophisticated and fluid continuum of use. Little progress has been made in attempts to create a model of senior center use, and the author would argue this is due in large part to pigeonholing elderly as either users or nonusers. Senior center use should be viewed as a dynamic process that ranges from potential utilization up to and through ex-utilization. The elderly who attend (or do not attend) senior centers do not stop changing or aging once they hit age sixty or sixty-five, yet studies of center attendance generally ignore this fact.

One of the major gaps in the understanding of senior center use has to do with variation in levels of participation. Very little is known about why some elders attend frequently and are involved in many center activities while others attend sporadically and in a limited way. Almost no attention has been paid to why center participants increase, decrease, or actually end their center involvement. The few studies that have looked at this subject generally focus on variation in frequency of use (number of visits to a center), not in level of involvement, stability, duration, or discontinuation of involvement.

In some ways quite a bit is known about who uses senior centers, but most of these user profiles are superficial, and based on local samples. Contradictory findings abound; it is clear that different senior centers attract somewhat different user populations. Indeed, it is interesting to ponder just how much of a levelling effect senior center operation and programming have on the variation in senior center user characteristics.

Some attention has been paid to finding out how senior center users differ from nonusers. Factors relating to demographics, health and well-being, accessibility, and social contact have all been investigated to some degree, but again, the results have been far from conclusive. Very little research has been directed toward uncovering the reasons and motivations for senior center attendance. Why do elderly with many of the same socio-demographic characteristics choose or not choose to become or stay involved with a senior center? Is it just that those who attend senior centers are joiners and more sociable? What happens to center participants when they drop out? How can this be prevented or delayed? The author would suggest that the answers to these questions are quite complex, and that more in-depth research on this topic is required.

As has been noted previously, examinations of senior center utilization and users must work to overcome both research design and theoretical deficiencies. Virtually every study of senior center users, for example, adopts different criteria for classifying users versus nonusers. There is no standard treatment of independent variables. In fact, there is often little consistency in the criteria used to designate an organization as a senior center. Almost every study is a one-time project and cross-sectional. These research design problems will have to be addressed before a coherent body of literature on senior centers can be assembled.

Researchers must also make strides of a theoretical nature. Much of the existing research, while informative, has made little effort to utilize sociological or social-psychological theory. There is a body of literature on who becomes involved in organized activities and volunteering, yet most studies of senior center users are descriptive and test fairly unsophisticated hypotheses. Both research design and theoretical shortcomings need to be improved upon if future studies are to generate findings of greater utility for practitioners as well as academicians.

CHAPTER SUMMARY

This chapter has focused on the characteristics of senior center users, the variation in their attendance patterns, and the factors that differentiate them from nonattenders. The study of user versus nonuser differences has been central to attempts by gerontologists to understand why some elderly persons utilize senior centers and others do not. As has been seen, however, the existing research is full of contradictory and inconsistent findings. Various socio-demographic characteristics, as well as health status, life satisfaction and morale, accessibility to center, and social contact factors have all received attention as potential predictors of senior center utilization.

Existing research suggests that the most consistent correlates of senior center use are health status and life satisfaction. Senior center users have been found to have less serious health problems than nonusers and higher levels of life satisfaction, thus supporting the argument that senior centers largely serve the well elderly. Social contact—the amount of interaction with family and friends—has been found to be both higher and lower for center attenders versus nonattenders. It has also been suggested that senior centers provide opportunities for confidant and other primary relationships, but gerontological observers are not of one mind on this issue. However, the importance of social activities and relationships and health factors are supported by findings from studies examining the reasons the elderly themselves give for center attendance. Socio-demographic variables are found to be related to center utilization, but the results vary considerably from study to study and do not support generalizations one way or the other.

This chapter has also noted that relatively little attention has been given to examining variation in attendance or participation—there is a difference—among senior center users, despite compelling conceptual and practical reasons to do so. Senior center use is seen as an either/or condition, not a continuum involving time, intensity, and frequency of attendance. Information on why seniors change their participation patterns over time and the conditions under which they cease attendance is particularly lacking.

Thus, there is much to learn about user versus nonuser differences, reasons for center participation, and variation in center attendance patterns. There is also a lack of research on the impact or consequences of senior center utilization, although there appears to be a general opinion among gerontological professionals that senior centers provide supportive and positive experiences. It is clear that the conceptualization and measurement of senior center participation, and the impact of that participation, need further refinement and study. A better understanding of the dynamics of center use will be needed if the many policy questions surrounding the role centers play in the lives of the elderly today, and should play tomorrow, are to be answered.

REFERENCES

Auerbach, A. (1976). The elderly in rural and urban areas. In L. H. Ginsberg (Ed.), *Social work in rural communities*. New York: Council on Social Work Education.

Bley, N., Goodman, M., Dye, D., & Harel, Z. (1972). Characteristics of aged participants in an age-segregated leisure program. *The Gerontologist, 12,* 368–370.

Carp, F. (1976). A senior center in public housing for the elderly. *The Gerontologist, 16,* 243–249.

Cryns, A. (1980). A needs assessment survey among elderly residents of the town of Amherst, New York. Report No. 1: Summary of major data trends. Unpublished manuscript, SUNY-Buffalo.

Daum, M. (1982). Preference for age-homogeneous versus age-heterogeneous social integration. *Journal of Gerontological Social Work, 4,* 41–54.

Demko, D. (1980). Utilization, attrition and the senior center. *Journal of Gerontological Social Work, 2,* 87–93.

Downing, R., and Copeland, E. (1980). Services for the black elderly. National or local problems? *Journal of Gerontological Social Work, 2,* 289–303.

Ferraro, K., & Cobb, C. (1988). Participation in multipurpose senior centers. *The Journal of Applied Gerontology, 6,* 429–447.

Frankel, G. (1966). The multipurpose senior citizens' center. A new comprehensive agency. *The Gerontologist, 6,* 23–27.

Freedman, R., & Axelrod, M. (1952). Who belongs to what in a metropolis. *Adult Leadership, 1,* 6–9.

Gelfand, D., & Gelfand, J. (1982). Senior centers and support networks. In D. Siegel and A. Naparstek (Ed.), *Community support systems and mental health.* New York: Springer Publishing Company.

Hanssen, A., Meima, N., Buckspan, L., Henderson, B., Helbig, T., & Zarit, S. (1978). Correlates of senior center participation. *The Gerontologist, 18,* 193–199.

Harris, L., & Associates, Inc. (1975). *The myth and reality of aging in America.* Washington, DC: National Council on the Aging.

Hoppa, M., & Roberts, G. (1974). Implications of the activity factor. *The Gerontologist, 14,* 331–335.

Krout, J. (1983a). Knowledge and use of services by the elderly: A critical review of the literature. *International Journal of Aging and Human Development, 17,* 9–23.

Krout, J. (1983b). Correlates of senior center utilization. *Research on Aging, 5,* 339–352.

Krout, J. (1983c). The organization, operation, and programming of senior centers: A national survey. Final report to the AARP Andrus Foundation. Fredonia, New York.

Krout, J. (1984). The organizational characteristics of senior centers in America. *Journal of Applied Gerontology, 3,* 192–205.

Krout, J. (1985). Senior center activities and services: Findings from a national survey. *Research on Aging, 7,* 455–471.

Krout, J. (1986). *The aged in rural America.* Westport, Connecticut: Greenwood Press.

Krout, J. (1988). The frequency, duration, stability, and discontinuation of senior center participation: Causes and consequences. Final report to the AARP Andrus Foundation. Fredonia, New York.

Krout, J. (1989). Area agencies on aging: Service planning and provision for the rural elderly. Final report to the Retirement Research Foundation. Fredonia, New York.

Krout, J., Cutler, S., & Coward, R. (1989). Correlates of senior center participation: A national analysis. Unpublished manuscript.

Leanse, J. & Wagener, S. (1975). Senior centers: A report of senior group programs in America. Washington, DC: National Council on the Aging.

Maxwell, J. (1962). Centers for older people: Guide for programs and facilities. Washington, DC: National Council on the Aging.

May, A., Herrman, S., & Fitzgerald, J. (1976). An evaluation of congregate meals programs and health of elders: Scott County and Fort Smith Arkansas, Bulletin No. 808, Fayetteville, University of Arkansas.

National Center for Health Statistics. Stone, R. (1986). Aging in the eighties, age 65 years and over—Use of community services; Preliminary data from the Supplement on Aging to the National Health Interview Survey: United States, January-June 1984. *Advance Data From Vital and Health Statistics*. No. 124, DHHS Pub. No. (PHS) 86–1250, September 30, Hyattsville, Maryland: Public Health Service.

Osgood, M. (1977). Rural and urban attitudes towards welfare. *Social Work, 22,* 41–47.

Powers, E., & Bultena, G. (1974). Correspondence between anticipated and actual use of public services by the aged. *Social Services Review, 48,* 245–254.

Ralston, P. (1984a). Senior center utilization by black elderly adults: Social, attitudinal, and knowledge correlates. *Journal of Gerontology, 39,* 224–229.

Ralston, P. (1984b). Senior center research: Concept, programs and utilization. Paper presented at the Annual Meeting of the Gerontological Society of America, San Antonio, Texas.

Ralston, P. (1985). Determinants of senior center attendance. Paper presented at the Annual Meeting of the Gerontological Society of America, New Orleans.

Ralston, P., & Griggs, M. (1985). Factors affecting utilization of senior centers. Race, sex and socioeconomic differences. *Journal of Gerontological Social Work, 9,* 99–111.

Rosen, C., Vandenberg, R., & Rosen, S. (1981). The fate of senior center dropouts. In P. Kim & C. Wilson (Eds.), *Toward mental health of the rural elderly*. Washington, DC: University Press of America.

Rosenzweig, N. (1975). Some differences between elderly people who use community resources and those who do not. *Journal of the American Geriatrics Society, 23,* 224–233.

Schramm W., & Storey, R. (1962). *Little house: A study of senior citizens*. Stanford: Institute for Communication Research.

Sela, I. (1986). A study of programs and services for the hearing impaired elderly in senior centers and clubs in the U.S. Unpublished dissertation. Washington, DC: Gallaudet College.

Silvey, R. (1962). Participation in a senior citizens day center. In J. Kaplan and G. J. Aldridge (Eds.), *Social welfare of the aging*. New York: Columbia University Press.

Storey, R. (1962). Who attends a senior activity center? A comparison of Little House members with non-members in the same community. *The Gerontologist, 2,* 216–222.

Taietz, P. (1970). *Community structure and aging*. Ithaca, NY: Cornell University.

Taietz, P. (1976). Two conceptual models of the senior center. *Journal of Gerontology, 31,* 219–222.

Tissue, T. (1971). Social class and the senior citizen center. *The Gerontologist, 11,* 196–200.

Toseland, R., & Sykes, J. (1977). Senior citizens center participation and other correlates of life satisfaction. *The Gerontologist, 17,* 235–241.

Trela, J. (1976). Social class and association membership: An analysis of age-graded and non-age graded voluntary participation. *Journal of Gerontology, 31,* 198–203.

Trela, J., & Simmons, L. (1971). Health and other factors affecting membership and attrition in a senior center. *Journal of Gerontology, 26,* 46–51.

Tuckman, J. (1967). Factors related to attendance in a center for older people. *Journal of American Geriatrics Society, 15,* 474–479.

7

Linkages and the Community
Services Network

INTRODUCTION

From their beginnings, senior centers have been places where older adults could congregate to socialize and to participate in a wide range of activities and services oriented to their needs, interests, and skills. One of the central goals of senior centers has been to help keep the elderly involved in the community. Thus, it should not be surprising that senior centers have forged working relationships and partnerships with a large number and variety of organizations in their communities.

This chapter takes a close look at the nature, scope, and impact of these working relationships. For want of a better term, these relationships are generally referred to as linkages, because they connect senior centers and their users to a broad range of organizations and people in the local community and beyond. Findings from several studies conducted by the author with national samples will be presented and discussed to inform the reader of the nature and operation of senior center linkages.

It is clear that virtually all groups and organizations in society maintain interactions with other groups and organizations. Families, businesses, government agencies, schools, and so on all have structured interactions with particular constellations of groups—this is the essence of social organization. Senior centers, then, can be expected to have such interactions or linkages with organizations whose primary or significant function involves older persons.

DIVERSITY OF LINKAGES

Linkage arrangements take many forms. Wagener and Carter (1982, 39) identify the following types of linkage arrangements:

—information sharing—exchange of information to promote understanding of agency mission and/or available services and eligibility requirements

—referral and follow-up—interagency contacts to connect a person with needed services and later contact to learn disposition of case

—joint outreach—a planned, unduplicated effort to reach unserved older people in a specific area or in a specifically defined group; when people are identified, they are informed about and linked to services

—joint staff training—joint participation in development of programs in areas of shared concern; shared information, problems and problem solving

—outstationed staff—one agency places its personnel in another's facility while retaining administrative control

—colocation—offices (and services) or more than one agency placed in a single facility

—case-service management/coordination—formal/informal management of client's progress through network of services to assure that he/she receives services due

—joint programming—collaborative efforts to create programmatic responses to specific needs

—joint planning—collaborative decision and policy making, possibly including joint funding, joint budgeting, joint projects

—purchase of service—contractual agreements between two autonomous agencies; one with funds, the other with capability to provide service

It would appear that as senior centers emerged from the 1960s and moved into the 1970s, a certain amount of linkage activity was already in place. Data collected in the early 1970s by the National Council on the Aging (Leanse and Wagener, 1975) illustrates this quite vividly. The NCOA study found that 34 percent of the senior centers in their survey reported directing referrals, and 32 percent receiving referrals, from Area Agencies on Aging. Forty percent of the centers indicated they exchanged information with such agencies, and 30 percent sent or received reports from them. Centers reported a wide range of working relationships with other groups: 31 percent trained other agency personnel; 36 percent trained students; 49 percent convened meetings of service agencies; 55 percent coordinated service delivery; 61 percent convened meetings of other aging groups; 67 percent cooperated in joint service delivery; 70 percent served as a resource to other community agencies; and 75 percent sponsored community-wide programs for the elderly. Only four percent of the centers reported no cooperative efforts. Educational institutions and nursing homes were most often cited as the cooperative parties (Leanse and Wagener, 1975).

A more recent study conducted by the National Institute of Senior Centers (Jacobs, 1980) focused on the role of senior centers in serving at-risk elderly. The findings of this study are limited because of the small sample size and low response rate, but are instructive nonetheless. Jacobs reports that 94 percent of the centers indicated they coordinate their services with other community agencies. Three-quarters of the respondents reported working with local social services, Social Security offices, legal services, and departments of public health. Two-thirds of the senior centers coordinated with religious organizations, hospitals, visiting nurse associations, and nursing homes (Jacobs, 1980).

The Older Americans Act and its amendments surely helped to fuel the spread of these activities, exchanges, and joint ventures. In particular, the 1978 introduction of the term focal point, as noted in previous chapters, explicitly drew attention to the role that local senior centers can and should play in bringing senior citizens in contact with the myriad of programs and agencies designed to meet their needs. Recall that the 1978 amendments required Area Agencies on Aging to designate focal points for comprehensive and coordinated service delivery to the elderly, and identified senior centers as worthy of special consideration for this status. Research by Wagener (1981) found that two-thirds of the organizations designated as focal points by AAAs were senior centers, and 27 percent were nutrition sites. A more recent study by the author found that two-thirds of the senior centers in a small national sample reported focal point status (Krout, 1987). Further, as a higher priority (and funding level) was given to existing services for the elderly and as new programs were developed, the linkage network of senior centers expanded. Unfortunately, it is difficult to empirically document this expansion during the 1970s because longitudinal data appropriate to do so are difficult to obtain.

The author's recent national survey of Area Agencies on Aging provides clear evidence that senior centers are part of the local community-based services system (Krout, 1989a). For example, AAA directors were asked to indicate the types and number of sites used to deliver services in their planning and service area (PSA). Almost all of the AAAs (92 percent) reported senior center delivery sites. The next most frequently noted site was a multipurpose community center (62 percent). The median number of senior centers used in delivery sites in a PSA was ten—a number that follow-up interviews revealed was under-reported. The median number of total delivery sites was twenty-three.

But the data on delivery sites understate the importance of senior centers in the aging services network. Discussions with AAA directors reveal that programs involving staff from other agencies and organizations utilize senior centers on a regular basis for many kinds of services. Many directors with multicounty, rural PSAs report that senior centers act as the hub of service provision and information for seniors with access, health, and social needs. Regardless of the mix of local versus AAA funding, senior centers generally have a considerable degree of visibility and support in these communities, and often serve as a major entry point into the service system (Krout, 1989a).

The author collected some information on senior center linkages from a national sample of senior centers in 1982 (Krout, 1983, 1986), and more detailed information from another national sample in 1986 (Krout, 1987, 1988, 1989b). The remainder of the chapter focuses on the findings from these studies, especially

Table 7.1
General Linkage Characteristics

Type of Relationship	Percent
Services Involving Linkages	
Few	24.9
Some	35.0
About half	18.1
Most	11.0
Almost all	11.0
Informal Linkages	
Few	22.0
Some	16.9
About half	13.5
Most	20.7
Almost all	27.0
Memos of Understanding	
Few	60.6
Some	22.0
About half	5.9
Most	5.9
Almost all	5.5
Contractual Relationships	
Few	79.8
Some	11.8
About half	4.2
Most	2.1
Almost all	2.1
Required by Sponsor	
Few	59.1
Some	21.5
About half	5.5
Most	6.3
Almost all	7.6
Most Effective Linkage Type	
Informal	53.2
Memo of understanding	24.1
Contractual	10.5
Required	12.3
General Senior Center Population	
Few	18.0
Some	31.8
About half	25.8
Most	17.2
Almost all	7.3
Low Income	
Few	9.4
Some	17.0
About half	22.6
Most	26.8
Almost all	24.3

Table 7.1 (continued)

Type of Relationship	Percent
Frail	
Few	26.0
Some	29.8
About half	16.6
Most	14.5
Almost all	13.2
Ethnic/Minority	
Few	58.3
Some	17.4
About half	7.7
Most	6.8
Almost all	9.8
Nutritional Needs	
Few	23.8
Some	27.2
About half	17.0
Most	17.4
Almost all	14.5

*N = 246
Source: J. Krout (1987). Senior center linkages and the provision of services to the elderly. Final report to the AARP Andrus Foundation. Fredonia, New York.

the most recent one. This project was specifically designed to examine multiple facets of senior center linkages with other organizations in the community. The findings are based on a forty-eight state random sample of 245 senior centers.

EXTENT OF AND REASONS FOR LINKAGES

Data on the degree to which this national sample of senior centers worked with other organizations in providing activities and services to their users in 1986 are presented in Table 7.1. One-quarter of the centers reported that their staff worked with only a few other organizations, while one-third indicated that some of their programming involved such relationships. Another 18 percent of the centers reported involving other organizations in about half of their offerings. Finally, one of five centers reported working with other organizations for most or almost all of the services they offered (Krout, 1989b).

Table 7.1 also presents general data on the kinds of working relationships senior centers develop with other organizations in their communities. Almost one-half of the centers characterize most or almost all of these working relationships as informal. More formal arrangements (memos of understanding, contracts) were reported to apply to only a few of the working relationships. Indeed, contractual agreements and memos of understanding were noted for only a few of the linkages by 80 percent and 61 percent of the respondents respectively. The same finding applies to linkages that are required by program guidelines or funding sources (Krout, 1989b).

As might be expected, informal linkages were seen as most effective by slightly more than one-half of the respondents. Memos of understanding were selected by one-quarter of the respondents, while contractual or required agreements were seen as most effective by only about 10 percent of the sample. The data also reveal that the majority of working relationships involving activities and services were not short-term. One-third of the respondents said the linkages continued for more than five years, while almost one-quarter said from two to five years. Only 13 percent indicated that these linkages lasted for only several months (Krout, 1989b).

Finally, data in Table 7.1 also show the degree to which linkage arrangements were targeted to particular groups of elderly senior center users. For one-half of the centers, only some of the linkage arrangements were seen as affecting the general senior center population. Another one-quarter of the respondents said that about half or almost all of the linkages were directed in this general manner. Degree of targeting was found to be very much alike for two other categories— nutritional needs and frail elderly. Here, 51 percent and 56 percent of respondents indicated that only few or some linkages were targeted to these areas and 32 percent and 28 percent most or almost all respectively. The group least likely to be targeted as part of linkage arrangements was ethnic/minority elderly. Such targeting was noted as involved with only a few linkages for almost 60 percent of the centers and some for another 17 percent. On the other hand, one-half of the centers indicated that most or almost all of their linkages involved low-income elderly, another 23 percent said about half, and 26 percent cited few or some working relationships on behalf of low-income elderly (Krout, 1989b).

These data indicate that linkages are entered into to affect senior center users in general, and especially low-income users. This should not be surprising since many, though not all, senior center users are of lower or lower middle income. Relatively few senior centers have large numbers of minority elderly, so this group is not targeted overall. Those senior centers that do have larger numbers of minority attenders no doubt see them as a linkage target group. It is somewhat surprising to find that one-quarter of the centers indicate targeting to the frail elderly account for most or almost all their linkages (Krout, 1989b).

Data in Table 7.1 indicate the degree to which, in general, senior centers have some form of working relationship with other organizations, and how these linkages can be characterized. Considerable variation is found for the overall degree of linkage involvement. To help understand the reasons for high versus low linkage levels, multiple regression analysis was performed for the overall degree to which center activities and services were reported to involve linkages. Measures of center, user, community, and director characteristics were used as independent variables.

The following variables were found to be significantly related to overall linkage activity: director's salary, age, and sex; subunit status; full-time paid staff; total number of services provided; and population size of area served. Thus, the regression analysis reveals that senior centers with a greater percentage of services involving linkages serve more populated areas, are more likely to be a focal point or a subunit of another organization, offer more services, have more full-time paid staff, have less well-paid and younger directors, and are more likely to have a male director. These independent variables explain almost 24 percent of the variation in overall linkage involvement (Krout, 1989b).

In addition to using multivariate statistical analysis, insight about linkages can be gained by asking senior center directors why they engage in these relationships with other organizations. This was done by the author in his 1986 national survey. The most frequently identified reason, given by 82 percent of respondents, was to better meet the needs of the elderly. The next most frequently identified reasons were increasing the number of services provided (80 percent) and elderly served (78 percent), and providing services for low-income or frail elderly (79 percent). Two-thirds of the sample indicated that carrying out focal point functions led them to linkage arrangements. Slightly more than one-half of the center directors said they worked with other organizations to assist them with their programming and because it was required by program guidelines. About 40 percent of the respondents indicated that a lack of staff expertise accounted for their involvement with other organizations. Only one-third mentioned a need to reduce operating expenses or a desire to increase referrals. Not surprisingly, the general response, "improving the ability to meet the needs of the elderly," was by far most often identified as the most important reason for linkages (53 percent), while increasing the number of elderly served was second (15 percent) and increasing the number of services provided (10 percent) was third (Krout, 1989b).

What can be concluded from these findings? The cross-sectional nature of the author's study makes the identification of causality difficult. It could well be that the availability of a greater number and variety of linkage partners in larger communities leads to more activity. Likewise, more staff resources would allow a center to develop and maintain linkages for more services. It should be recognized that setting up and maintaining linkages can involve costs in areas such as staff time, supplies, and transportation, and can result in increased demand for services by participants (Krout, 1986).

At the same time, it would also seem reasonable to expect that senior centers with more involvement in linkages would be likely to attract participants through more diverse and better service offerings. As attendance increases, senior center directors can better justify and bargain for more resources for their center. Linkages, then, can serve as both a cause and an effect of senior center resources and services, providing that the resources and linkage partners are available. Variables such as community size, center staff, and director characteristics serve at least to some extent as necessary, but not sufficient, conditions for significant linkage activity (Krout, 1986).

However, the data reveal that senior centers with similar characteristics have quite different levels of linkage involvement. The goals of the center participants and directors, and their expectations of what and who the center should be involved with, appear to play a significant role in determining linkages. These goals may account for the variation found among senior centers with similar structural characteristics. Recall that data on senior center goals, reported in chapter three, revealed that a very small percentage of senior center directors identify linkages as a goal. Linkages are engaged in as a means to achieve the major goals of senior centers, such as providing services and improving the quality of life and self-image of aging. Some of the specific goals noted by senior center directors are more apt to require or be affected by linkage activity than others. For example, promoting friendship among center participants might require little linkage activity, while providing legal services might require working with local attornies or a legal services corporation. Again, centers may choose to work toward their goals with more or less involvement with other organizations, and they are limited by the organizational environment of the surrounding community (Krout, 1989b).

The data presented on linkage reasons may provide additional insight here. Recall that the most frequently identified reasons involved increasing services and the number of elderly served, and meeting the needs of the elderly, especially target groups of low-income and frail. Greater linkage activity could be expected where these reasons are consistent with or reflect senior center goals or philosophy. The characteristics of center directors also have an impact on overall linkage activity. Thus it is not just a matter of goals and resources, but also of who is in the director's position (Krout, 1989b).

The data show that the linkage process is fairly widespread, and usually informal. This finding sheds some additional light on the question of why senior centers engage in linkages. It would appear that they do not do so because they have to, or because it has become a contractual obligation. Rather, linkages help center staff do their work. The informal type of linkage is seen as the most effective, with another less formal linkage, memos of understanding, a distant second. It should not be surprising that the most widespread linkage type is also seen as the most effective.

LINKAGE ORGANIZATIONS

It is clear that senior centers utilize linkages with other organizations in their day-to-day operation. Findings from the NCOA study (Leanse and Wagener, 1975) on specific kinds of linkage activities and from Jacobs (1980) on some of the organizations involved in this process have already been reviewed. This section provides a detailed look at this topic from the author's study of senior center linkages (Krout, 1987, 1988). Table 7.2 shows the percentage of senior centers in the sample reporting major types of linkage activity with various organizations.

Sending referrals to other agencies is the most common linkage activity. At least half of the senior centers in the study reported sending referrals to the following organizations: social security or health departments, nutrition sites, other senior centers, county social services, visiting nurses or home health agencies, hospitals, private physicians, housing authorities, legal aid, and county offices for the aging. About 40 percent of the centers refer to nursing homes, parks and recreation departments, caseworkers, human services agencies, religious organizations, and state and county offices on aging, while only about one-quarter of the centers send referrals to health maintenance organizations, schools, special disability groups, and chambers of commerce. The three organizations least likely to receive referrals from senior centers are employment security commissions, youth groups, and unions. The mean number of organizations involved with center referrals is 10.1 and the median is 10.5 (Krout, 1988).

A similar pattern of activity is found for the receipt of referrals from other organizations; however, the percentages are generally somewhat smaller than for sending referrals to organizations. Overall, a close correspondence is found between the percentage of senior centers indicating referrals to and from other organizations. Presumably, centers that engage in one type of referral with an organization engage in the other as well. The mean number of organizations sending referrals to senior centers is 8.7 and the median is 7.9 (Krout, 1988).

A somewhat smaller percentage of respondents indicated planning and coordinating the delivery of services with other organizations. For the most part, only one-third of the centers reported such a working relationship with organizations other than state and county offices for the aging, senior centers, and nutrition sites. Organizations such as local offices of aging, health departments, parks and recreation, county social services, and legal aid were cited as planning/ coordination partners by only 20 to 30 percent of the centers. Less than one in five senior centers reported linkages with caseworkers or private physicians, organizations such as human service agencies, housing authorities or religious groups. The mean number of organizations senior centers planned and coordinated service delivery with was 4.7, and the median was 2.7 (Krout, 1988).

Only a small percentage of senior centers reported formal agreements with any of the organizations. The exceptions (State Units on Aging, AAAs) involve agencies that provide funding for some of the services offered by senior centers. Informal agreements are found for considerably higher percentages of the centers. About one-third of the centers have informal agreements with county social services, local social security and health departments, hospitals, visiting nurse and home health organizations, other senior centers, human service agencies, and religious organizations. A somewhat smaller percentage of the senior centers report informal agreements with county aging agencies, private physicians, local recreation and parks departments, nursing homes, housing authorities, nutrition sites, caseworkers, service clubs, legal aid, schools, and libraries. The mean number of organizations with which centers have informal and formal linkages is 5.8 and 2.4, while the median is 3.2 and 1.8, respectively (Krout, 1988).

These data clearly indicate that some organizations are more likely to be worked with in general than others. County offices for the aging, local health,

Table 7.2
Senior Center Linkages with Other Organizations*

Agencies/ Organizations	Referrals to	from	Planning and Coordination of Service Delivery	Formal Agreement (Contract, memo of understanding)	Informal Agreement (Verbal)
State office on aging	38.7	37.8	35.5	41.5	14.7
County Agencies on Aging	45.6	47.0	38.2	34.6	21.2
Local office on aging	32.7	33.2	27.2	29.0	13.8
Local Social Security	60.8	36.9	13.8	4.6	32.7
County social services	57.1	48.4	27.2	12.4	31.3
Local health department	60.4	44.7	29.5	12.0	36.9
Chamber of commerce	26.7	20.7	7.4	2.3	18.9
Private physicians	47.0	45.6	12.9	2.3	29.0
Hospitals	50.2	53.0	25.8	10.1	37.8
Local parks & recreation	39.6	32.7	27.2	9.2	27.6
Visiting nurses/ Home health	62.7	53.5	26.3	12.9	33.6
Health maintenance orgs.	23.5	18.0	7.8	4.1	13.4
Nursing homes	43.4	36.4	12.4	3.2	23.0
Housing authorities	52.5	37.8	13.8	4.6	26.7
Senior centers	59.9	54.4	32.3	8.8	32.7
Nutrition sites	63.6	52.5	34.6	23.5	26.3
Daycare centers	29.5	21.2	8.3	6.0	14.7
Casework/Case management	43.8	35.5	16.6	9.2	20.7
Unions	2.8	2.3	0.9	0.0	3.7
Human services agencies (Y's, Salvation Army)	43.3	40.1	18.0	5.5	30.0
Religious organizations	46.5	47.9	18.4	2.8	30.9
Service clubs	32.3	32.7	14.3	1.4	24.4
Youth groups	14.3	14.3	7.8	1.4	12.0
Legal Aid	55.3	37.8	19.4	11.1	26.3
Employment Security Comm.	17.5	13.8	3.7	2.8	9.2
Schools	27.6	25.3	18.0	9.2	20.3
Special disability groups	25.3	23.0	9.2	1.8	18.9

Table 7.2 (continued)

Agencies/ Organizations	Referrals to	Referrals from	Plannning and Coordination of Service Delivery	Formal Agreement (Contract, memo of understanding)	Informal Agreement (Verbal)
Library	35.0	29.5	17.5	3.7	24.4

*All numbers in percents.

Source: J. Krout (1988). Senior center linkages with community organizations. *Research on Aging*, 10, 258–274. Reprinted by permission of Sage Publications, Inc.

social services and parks and recreation departments, other senior centers, nutrition sites, religious organizations, hospitals, housing authorities, legal aid, and casework agencies are most important in regard to referrals and service planning and coordination. It is interesting to note that in some instances the prevalence of such organizational involvement is less than one might expect. For example, slightly less than one-third of the senior centers in the sample report planning coordination activity with county agencies on aging. Yet two-thirds of the centers indicate they have been designated as focal points by these Area Agencies on Aging. This apparent inconsistency might be accounted for by the fact that both county and local aging offices were listed on the survey. Combining the percentages of these two almost doubles the proportion of senior centers reporting such linkages. Or it might be that focal point status for senior centers exists in some cases in name but not function (Krout, 1988).

On the other hand, some of the percentages are higher than might be expected. For example, almost one-half of the centers note linkages through referrals to private physicians, and approximately one-quarter work with health maintenance organizations, chambers of commerce, and daycare centers. Not surprising, and particularly telling, is the very low percentage of senior centers that report working with youth groups. In addition, the data reveal that referral activity is the most prevalent form of linkage arrangement for every organization specifically identified in the survey. This would seem to support the thesis that one of the central roles played by senior centers is that of information and referral. This function, along with providing services to elderly participants directly, defines what senior centers do. They function much less as planning and coordinating organizations (Krout, 1988).

LINKAGE SERVICES AND TYPES OF ASSISTANCE

This examination of linkage activity now includes information on the general degree of senior center involvement and the reasons for it, linkage targeting, and the organizations senior centers work with. Two more pieces of information

Table 7.3
Linkage Activity for Specific Services

Service	Percent of Centers Providing Services	Percent of Centers Working with Other Organizations	Mean Number of Other Organizations
Information & Assistance			
Consumer information	72.4	58.3	3.1
Crime prevention	61.5	79.7	1.4
Financial/taxes	77.5	76.7	1.5
Housing information	65.8	64.1	1.7
Legal aid	67.1	82.1	1.2
Public assistance	49.4	80.0	1.6
Programs (SSI, food stamps, etc.)	62.3	84.8	1.6
Social security & medicare	67.5	79.0	1.4
Mean for Information Assistance	65.4	75.6	1.7
Personal Counseling & Mental Health Services			
Crisis intervention	34.6	76.5	1.5
Group counseling	32.5	61.8	1.5
Individual counseling	49.8	62.9	1.6
Peer counseling	27.3	57.1	1.2
Mean for Counseling	36.1	64.6	1.5
Special Services			
Adult day care/adhc	22.5	58.5	1.7
Crisis & emergency service	32.5	67.1	1.7
Programs for disabled	31.6	60.3	1.6
Protective services	34.6	86.3	1.3
Nursing home programs	31.6	71.2	2.0
Mean for Special Services	30.6	68.7	1.7
Access to Center			
Information/referral	75.9	43.1	2.0
Outreach	71.5	37.1	1.4
Transportation	83.3	55.0	1.3
Mean for Access	76.9	45.1	1.6
Health and Nutrition			
Screening & maintenance	63.6	52.3	1.7
Health education/health counseling	66.8	72.1	1.8
Nutrition education/ nutrition counseling	73.8	64.5	1.5
Group meals	83.8	56.0	1.4
Home delivered meals	70.3	57.8	1.1
Mean for Health & Nutrition	71.7	62.5	1.5
In-Home Services			
Escort	46.3	39.6	1.2
Friendly visiting	58.5	42.5	1.1
Homemaker	45.4	68.3	1.3
Home health care	37.7	75.9	1.6
Home repair/winterization	49.6	79.8	1.2
Telephone/TYY/TDD reassurance	47.8	42.2	1.2
Chore/handy man	35.5	50.6	1.1
Mean for In-Home Services	45.8	57.9	1.2

Table 7.3 (continued)

Service	Percent of Centers Providing Services	Percent of Centers Working With Other Organizations	Mean Number of Other Organizations
Income Supplement			
Craft shops	34.5	20.3	1.0
Discount program	21.9	62.0	1.2
Food coop	9.2	61.9	1.0
Small appliance repair	5.3	33.3	1.0
Thrift shop	19.3	29.5	2.0
Job training	21.9	80.0	1.3
Job placement	29.8	69.1	1.3
Mean for Income Supplement	20.3	50.9	1.3
Case Management			
Advocacy	42.1	44.8	1.8
Assessment	37.3	42.4	1.6
Outreach	48.7	37.8	1.5
Counseling	41.7	43.2	1.7
Information/referral	58.3	41.0	2.1
Mean for Case Management	45.6	41.8	1.7

Source: J. Krout (1988). Senior center linkages with community organizations
Research on Aging, 10, 258-274. Reprinted by permission of
Sage Publications, Inc.

will add substantially to this picture—the particular senior center services where linkages are involved, and the specific nature of the assistance or exchange involved in the working relationship.

Table 7.3 presents data on the percentage of senior centers that have linkages involving specific services with other organizations. The data in the first column show the percentage of the centers in the sample that offered each service. The second column shows the percentage of these centers that have working relationships with other organizations involving each service, and the third column indicates the mean number of linkage organizations for each service.

With the exception of a few individual services, 60 to 70 percent of the centers that provide services in the information and assistance, personal counseling and mental health, special services, health and nutrition, and in-home categories work with at least one other organization. Forty to 50 percent of the centers offering access to center, income supplement, and case management programs work with others. The data also reveal that senior centers work with an average of less than two organizations. Considerable variation is found for another indicator of linkage activity—the degree to which senior centers are self-sufficient in regard to providing specific services. For example, about three-quarters of the centers offering information and assistance services work with other organizations. Several types of services that are offered by a small percentage of centers—income supplement, mental health, and special services—also usually involve linkages (Krout, 1988).

These data clearly show that some services are more likely to be involved in the linkage process than others. For example, the provision of most information and assistance services involves linkages. This probably reflects the nature of the service, as well as the training of center staff—they may not have the expertise to provide the needed information themselves. Staff expertise and availability may also account for the large percentage of centers that rely on outside assistance for services such as home repair, home health care, job training, and protective services.

It should be kept in mind that senior centers generally are not designed to provide all of these services by themselves, nor should it be their job to do so. After all, many communities have agencies that specialize in certain types of services. The data, general as it is, does show that the majority of senior centers offering services work with other organizations most of the time in assisting their users. They function in the service network as a linking organization themselves. It is also clear that out of necessity, choice, and probably need, senior centers work with only a small number of organizations. Often only one or two are available, and are all that are needed (Krout, 1988).

Finally, data on the types of assistance or exchanges senior centers are involved with are presented in Table 7.4. These data are for those senior centers that work with at least one other organization in providing services to the elderly. While the percentage of centers varies for different services, the most prevalent type of working relationships are providing staff on-site, sharing information, and sending or taking referrals. Generally, less than 15 percent of the centers report providing space off-site, training center staff, and transportation (Krout, 1987).

LINKAGE BARRIERS

Another facet of senior center linkages has to do with the level and types of difficulties encountered in carrying out these working relationships. Again, the author's national study has addressed this issue. Data in Table 7.5 show the percentage of senior centers experiencing specific difficulties in working with other organizations. From one-half to two-thirds of the centers report seldom having difficulties for most of the problem types noted in the study. Lack of funding, transportation, participation by the elderly, time, and qualified staff are identified by the largest percentage of senior centers as causing problems at least some of the time. Twenty percent of the centers indicate that a lack of funding causes difficulties most of the time or always, while 14 percent of the centers note this for lack of transportation. Only a very small percentage of centers have discontinued a linkage arrangement because of any of the problems—6 percent, for lack of funding, is the highest amount (Krout, 1987).

To provide a general picture of linkage problems, each senior center was given a summed problem score. If a center indicated that a particular problem was seldom experienced, the center was scored as zero for that problem. Otherwise,

Table 7.4
Type of Linkage Activity

Service Category	Provide Staff On-Site	Provide Staff Off-Site	Type of Involvement Provide Space Off-Site	Train Staff	Share Information	Provide Transportation	Send/take Referrals
Information assistance	35.4	19.8	7.9	8.0	42.9	4.9	34.7
Personal counseling and mental health	41.6	27.3	12.7	11.5	30.8	7.0	37.7
Special services	21.8	26.3	10.3	9.1	37.0	15.6	46.4
Access to center	34.0	13.1	3.9	11.2	22.6	23.3	23.0
Health and nutrition	48.9	18.2	7.5	13.8	32.3	12.4	29.6
In-home services	25.8	23.2	5.8	7.1	24.6	10.2	34.9
Income supplement	23.6	21.5	9.5	9.5	32.7	4.3	28.6
Case management	31.4	16.4	5.6	10.8	24.9	8.2	25.8

*Only centers that work with at least one other organization in providing services.

Source: J. Krout (1987). Senior center linkages and the provision of services to the elderly. Final report to the AARP Andrus Foundation. Fredonia, New York.

Table 7.5
Problems Experienced in Linkage Arrangements

Difficulty	Seldom	Some of the Time	About Half of the Time	Most of the Time	Always	Discontin-uation of Linkage
			Frequency*			
Turf protection	68.8	20.5	4.7	4.7	1.4	2.3
Lack of transportation	47.5	27.9	11.2	9.3	4.2	1.4
Goal differences	78.6	17.7	2.8	0.9	0.0	0.5
Procedural differences	70.7	23.7	3.7	1.9	0.0	0.9
Personality conflicts	76.3	19.1	4.7	0.0	0.0	1.4
Lack of time	56.1	24.3	13.6	4.2	1.9	0.9
Staff turnover	73.0	19.1	5.6	1.4	0.9	1.9
Inadequate facilities	67.0	24.2	4.7	2.3	1.9	1.9

Lack of communication	62.8	26.5	6.5	3.7	0.5	1.9
Disagreement about needs of the elderly	81.0	14.9	3.7	0.5	0.0	0.0
Lack of funding	34.9	30.7	14.9	10.7	8.8	6.5
Lack of participation by the elderly	49.3	35.8	10.7	3.3	0.9	3.3
Lack of qualified staff to organize/run program	58.2	29.3	7.4	3.3	1.9	2.8
Culture & language	98.1	0.5	0.0	0.5	0.5	0.0
Other	98.6	0.5	0.0	0.5	0.5	0.0

*All numbers in percents.

Source: J. Krout (1987). Senior center linkages and the provision of services to the elderly. Final report to the AARP Andrus Foundation. Fredonia, New York.

a center would receive a score of one. A total of fifteen possible problem areas were used, thus a linkage problem score can range from zero to fifteen. One-quarter of the senior centers reported no linkage problems; 22 percent indicated one to three; 24 percent had four to six; and 21 percent noted from seven to ten. Six percent of the senior centers report eleven or more problems (Krout, 1987).

Overall, the data indicate that senior centers do not encounter a large degree of difficulty in working with other organizations in the community. The mean and median number of problems identified by senior centers is about four out of a total of fifteen. However, some problems do exist. Of the many difficulties identified in the survey, lack of funding, transportation, participation by the elderly, time, and qualified staff are noted by the largest percentage of senior centers. Most of these reflect a lack of adequate resources to maintain linkages. In fact, lack of funding is clearly the most often noted difficulty, yet only 6 percent of the centers report that this problem has forced the discontinuation of a linkage (Krout, 1987).

These findings suggest that more linkage activity would be engaged in by senior centers if they had more of the resources noted above. The problems with funding, transportation, and the rest have direct implications for the ability of centers to initiate and sustain the kinds of linkages examined here. Inadequate transportation could restrict the ability of a center to work in the referral area, for example. Lack of time—presumably staff time—is also cited by a relatively large number of centers. Both of these would appear to reflect center resources, such as budget, and to be particularly problematic for smaller centers. Nonprivate transportation has been noted by many observers as particularly lacking in rural areas.

Data not reported here also show that problems and barriers involved in coordination are related to some of the same variables that are related to linkages. Interestingly, the centers with larger budgets or located in larger communities that have linkages with more organizations also report experiencing a greater number of problems with linkages. It seems ironic that centers reporting more problems work with a larger number of organizations and have presumably overcome obstacles to such interaction. Rural and smaller centers are less able to support linkage activities due to a lack of resources or an absence of other organizations in the area, but report fewer problems with the working relationships they do have (Krout, 1987).

In sum, a wide range of factors impede the development of linkages between senior centers and other organizations. An increase in senior center resources, communication, and understanding should lead to an increase in linkages. If this be the case, current levels of linkages do not represent an optimal state and would be higher if these problems were reduced. Yet greater interaction between centers and other organizations may generate other problems.

LINKAGE CHANGES

The last aspect of senior center linkages to be considered is their recent and expected change. Data from the author's study reveal that the number of organizations with which centers form linkages were reported to have increased over the past several years for 62 percent of centers, and to have remained the same for one-third. The number of linkage organizations decreased for only 5 percent of the centers. The number of linkage arrangements, on the other hand, has stayed the same for one-half of the centers, and has increased for slightly less than half, while decreasing for only 4 percent. Finally, the number of linkages is expected to increase in the near future for one-half of the centers, remain the same for 40 percent, and decrease for 9 percent. Thus, the number of linkage arrangements and organizations involved with senior centers has increased in recent years, and is expected to increase or at least remain the same in the next few years (Krout, 1987).

Reasons for the increase in linkages were also solicited from center directors in the author's study. No data on linkage decreases were collected because so few centers noted this type of change. The most important reasons identified for the increase in the number of linkage organizations include: increased communication and cooperation (12 percent); greater recognition of the need for services and greater recognition of senior centers (11 percent); new or expanded programs (9 percent); improved or increased staff (8 percent); increases in the number of elderly (6 percent); and increases in the number of service offerings, preventing duplication, and improving nutrition programs (5 percent each) (Krout, 1987).

Center directors were not asked to identify a single most important reason for future increases in the number of linkage organizations, just to specify three reasons for anticipated change. The reason cited by the largest percentage of respondents for an increase in linkages in the future was the increase in the number of the elderly (18 percent). Other reasons noted include: increase in the number of services offered (10 percent); greater recognition and need for service, and new or expanded programs (9 percent each); greater recognition of senior centers, and an increase in communication and cooperation (5 percent each; Krout, 1987).

RESEARCH QUESTIONS

The information reviewed in this chapter has touched on a number of aspects of senior center linkages. Yet, only the surface of most of these issues has been scratched. The amount of attention paid by gerontological researchers to the form and process of these working relationships is almost negligible. The answers to a number of questions are needed if a greater understanding of the linkage topic is to be gained.

The linkages senior centers have developed attest to their flexibility, strength, and ability to work with other organizations. Nevertheless, it is relevant to call for an assessment of the level of linkage activity—is it low, high, or about right? This is difficult to determine because there is no conceptual or empirical point of comparison. Based on the available research, it can be said with some certainty whether a particular senior center has a higher or lower level of linkage involvement compared to other centers. But no nationally legislated guidelines or requirements, or even unofficial suggestions exist in this regard, and the data themselves support a wide range of interpretations (Krout, 1989b). While referral activity is fairly common, planning or coordination with county or local AAAs—the very agencies that presumably would be most involved in this kind of interaction—is much less evident. One could conclude that linkage components of the elderly service network are not as widespread as the past legislation intended, or as many gerontological researchers have suggested they should be (Estes, 1979; Soldo, 1980).

On the other hand, it could be argued that significant levels of linkage activity are shown by the data and that these levels reflect what senior centers and other organizations are currently willing and/or able to support, given all the other factors that impinge on their operation. The mutually preferred mode of linkage may be referral activity rather than colocation or planning or coordination. The difficulty of interpretation stems from a lack of more detailed data and the conceptual ambiguity of the focal point and linkage concepts. Researchers must pay more attention to these issues if they are to be resolved.

The relationship between senior center linkages and focal point activity must also continue to be examined. What kinds of linkages are desirable or necessary for maintaining senior center focal point status? What should the goals of such linkages be? Are linkages necessary for focal point success or can self-contained organizations serve as focal points? What type and amount of resources are needed to carry out focal point roles? Factors related to linkage change are also poorly understood (Krout, 1986).

Another issue involves the meaning of terms such as referral, coordination, and formal. When does contact with another agency become formal, or involve coordination? A center may plan its activities based on knowledge of what other organizations do—a kind of informal coordination—as opposed to working out more formalized agreements. Does sending referrals involve planning? The terminology used in future research should be developed with care (Krout, 1986).

In addition to the need for greater refinement of concepts used in linkage research and for more research based on these concepts, attention should also be directed to the effectiveness and impact of linkages on senior centers and their users. What impact do linkages, especially informal ones, have on senior center organization, staff, and users? Does working on linkages in reality constitute the most desirable use of staff time? What linkage costs and benefits exist community and system wide? How can such linkages be expanded and improved? What makes a good linkage? What variables are most strongly related to the quantity and quality of linkage activity? The existing research has not found any particular variable or set of variables to be consistently strong predictors of these factors. Finally, more attention should be given to understanding the nature of the barriers and problems involved in linkage activity, and the ways in which they can be prevented or managed most effectively. Much remains to be uncovered about the nature and consequences of the various types of working relationships senior centers across the nation have developed in their communities.

CHAPTER SUMMARY

The data presented in this chapter show that, on average, senior centers in the United States work with a fairly large number and range of organizations to provide services to their regular users as well as to other elderly in the community. But this general conclusion does not capture the large amount of variation and diversity that characterizes the linkage phenomenon. Senior centers are much more likely to report linkages with some organizations than others, and the likelihood of a linkage with an organization depends on the nature of the linkage. Whether or not centers maintain working relationships with other organizations also depends on the particular service involved. Overall, however, the data indicate that for most services, the majority of senior centers do in fact maintain some form of linkage. In doing so, they are able to make available, either directly or through referral, a wide range of services to their elderly participants.

Thus, it can be concluded that the majority of senior centers act as linking organizations in the service network. Either because of necessity, choice, or need, senior centers work with a small number of organizations in these linkage instances. Referral activity is the most prevalent form of linkage arrangement for every organization and is much more prevalent than planning and coordination. This finding supports the thesis that many senior centers play important information and referral roles—functions central to focal point status. Providing referrals and services directly to the elderly are two of the contributions senior centers make to the aging services network (Krout, 1988).

It is also of note that while senior centers do experience difficulties as part of the linkage process, these problems rarely lead to a discontinuation of the working relationship. The biggest problems appear to be lack of funding and lack of staff. Presumably, greater resources in these areas would allow even greater involvement with other organizations. These problems should not be ignored, because they do affect a significant percentage of centers. This suggests that greater efforts should be directed to teaching senior center and other organization staff how to make the most of available resources, and how linkages can be most effectively developed and maintained.

The author's research suggests the variation in the quantity of linkages is not adequately explained by the structural indicators of community, center, and center user demographics. Considerably more work needs to be carried out on uncovering the factors responsible for the linkage process. The key word here may well be "process." The author's data are from a national random sample of senior centers, and should have a high degree of generalizability. On the other hand, this research is cross-sectional and retrospective; it constitutes a snapshot of a phenomenon that is fluid, changeable, and subject to many factors not easily identified or measured through survey research. Participant observation and case studies may provide important insights into the linkage process. Ideally, researchers should strive to develop a typology of linkage relationships that can guide further efforts to uncover why some centers develop different levels and types of linkages, how they do so, and the impacts these linkages have for the senior center organizations and elderly service users involved (Krout, 1988).

As will be demonstrated in the next chapter, the role senior centers play in the community services network has not been well documented empirically and a better understanding of linkages between senior centers and the community is an important piece of that puzzle. Linkage activity can be seen as a component of the focal point concept. Assuming, as federal legislation does, that linkages are beneficial to the elderly and the service system, more should be learned about them so they can be expanded and improved.

REFERENCES

Estes, C. (1979). *The aging enterprise*. San Francisco: Jossey-Bass Publishers.

Jacobs, B. (1980). Senior centers and the at-risk older person. Washington, DC: National Council on the Aging.

Krout, J. (1983). The organization, operation, and programming of senior centers: A national survey. Final report to the AARP Andrus Foundation. Fredonia, New York.

Krout, J. (1986). Senior center linkages in the community. *The Gerontologist, 26,* 510–515.

Krout, J. (1987). Senior center linkages and the provision of services to the elderly. Final report to the AARP Andrus Foundation. Fredonia, New York.

Krout, J. (1988). Senior center linkages with community organizations. *Research on Aging, 10,* 258–274.

Krout, J. (1989a). Area agencies on aging: Service planning and provision for the rural elderly. Final report to the Retirement Research Foundation. Fredonia, New York.

Krout, J. (1989b). The nature and correlates of senior center linkages. *The Journal of Applied Gerontology, 8,* 307–322.

Leanse, J., & Wagener, L. (1975). Senior centers: A report of senior group programs in America. Washington, DC: National Council on the Aging.

Soldo, B. (1980). America's elderly in the 1980's. *Population Bulletin, 35.*

Wagener, L. (1981). The concept of a focal point for service delivery in the field of aging. Washington, DC: National Council on the Aging.

Wagener, L., & Carter, P. (1982). Building community partnerships. Washington, DC: National Council on the Aging.

8

Programming and Policy Issues

INTRODUCTION

Many of the topics discussed in the previous chapters have bearing on policy and planning issues for senior centers in particular and the aging services network in general. The purpose of this chapter is to identify and develop these policy issues. Perhaps the major policy-related question is how and where senior center activities fit into the community-based service system for the elderly. A consideration of this question involves examining not only what senior centers do, but how effectively it is done and who they serve. The answers to these questions are not entirely clear because this system (perhaps collection is a better term) is constantly changing in both size and function. It is a system whose direction fundamentally is driven by the availability of resources, while the resources presumably reflect the service demands and needs among the elderly. But the level and nature of resource allocations reflect political and ideological stances as well.

The 1980s have witnessed significant changes in health and social policy and funding. These changes have had considerable impact on senior centers. The first of these changes is the general diminishment under the Reagan administration of federal monies for social services. The second is the adoption of Diagnostic Related Groups (DRGs) in the Medicare reimbursement program, which has led to shorter hospital stays and more outpatient procedures, resulting in increased demand for in-home supportive health and related services (Binner, 1986; Weiss, 1986). The third change is the increasing focus of the Older Americans Act and many states on the frail or at-risk elderly, and on comprehensive service coordination at the local level (for example, focal points and care management). A full consideration of all the aging policy issues related to senior centers is beyond the scope of this book. However, this chapter does attempt to raise and place in clearer focus (at least from the author's perspective) the major policy issues involving senior centers.

FOCAL POINTS AND THE COMMUNITY BASED SERVICES SYSTEM

Data presented in previous chapters have shown that senior centers provide a wide range of programming to a relatively large number of elderly. Senior centers have been identified in the Older Americans Act as appropriate focal points for the coordination and delivery of comprehensive services for the elderly; many senior centers maintain linkages with numerous agencies and organizations that provide a wide array of support services for the noninstitutionalized elderly. But what contributions do senior centers really make to the aging services network?

One reasonable point of departure in considering this question is the focal point concept. Amendments to the Older Americans Act in both 1973 and 1978 contained language on focal points (Wagener, 1981), and the final regulations implementing the 1987 amendments, published by the Administration on Aging, included new language requiring Area Agencies on Aging to designate one or more "focal points on aging" in each community. As in the past, the regulations state that "special consideration" be given to "developing and/or designating multipurpose senior centers as community focal points on aging." The regulations further direct that Area Agencies on Aging "assure that community leadership work . . . with other applicable agencies and institutions in the community to achieve maximum colocation at, coordination with or access to other services and opportunities for the elderly from the designated community focal points" (U.S. Department of Health and Human Services, 1988).

The idea behind this concept is to reduce service fragmentation by designating key community organizations, such as senior centers, as places where services and information on them can be accessed by the elderly in a single location that is both visible and acceptable to them. Senior centers designated as focal points, then, have organizational identities and functions that are somewhat different from centers not so designated. The focal point concept implies a central position, in terms of horizontal and vertical linkages, for multipurpose senior centers in the aging services network, and it elevates their role as service delivery sites for Area Agencies on Aging.

Research findings presented in chapter seven indicate that over the years senior centers have indeed taken on a focal point identity in the eyes and actions of AAAs. It has been argued that senior centers often serve as the organizational hub of a larger network of community services for the elderly (Leanse, 1977), and the previous chapter has demonstrated that centers do work with a large array of organizations at the local level. Indeed, the author's ongoing study of AAAs has found that senior centers, far more than other organizations, serve as a delivery site or location for services to the elderly (Krout, 1989). An earlier study found that 41 percent of all AAA grants were delivered through multi-purpose senior centers and community centers (National Association of State Units on Aging, 1983). But the nature and scope of actual AAA funding and support for senior centers as focal points varies considerably. In some cases, AAAs provide dollars for senior center facilities, programming, and staff (program coordinators, outreach and in-home service workers). Some senior centers, especially in rural areas, are the dominant, central point of service delivery and information/referral for the AAA. Other AAAs provide little more than program dollars to senior centers, sometimes by choice but often because of limited resources and the increasing demand for in-home services for the frail and homebound.

The reliance on senior centers as focal points by AAAs stems from many factors other than the specific regulations of the Older Americans Act. Some centers predate AAAs; many others were developed or expanded in the early 1970s with grants from AAAs. Most senior centers grew out of and are based on community support. As pointed out earlier in this book, much of their funding comes from local and state sources, and senior centers are generally well-recognized and accepted organizational entities.

Nonetheless, the question that begs asking is, to what degree and how well do senior centers really function as focal points for the elderly? A definitive answer is most difficult because there are few existing empirical or conceptual yardsticks with which to make this determination. Neither the activities nor the outcomes necessary for focal point status have been clearly delineated or put into operation. Indeed, it can be argued that such yardsticks are inappropriate because focal point activities vary according to the economic, social, geographic, and organizational environment in which centers operate.

One reference point would be the 1978 Older Americans Act amendments, in which senior centers were identified as appropriate and desirable service delivery focal points. Recall that two-thirds of the senior centers in the author's study indicated that they had been officially designated as a focal point (Krout, 1987). Other data discussed in chapter seven, however, would seem to temper the conclusion that the majority of centers are functioning as focal points. The focal point concept can be likened to what the seminal sociologist Max Weber called an ideal type. An ideal type does not describe any actual phenomenon, but rather something to be strived for that describes the essential characteristics of a subject, and that can be used to compare and analyze existing things (Weber, 1947).

One way to approach this question is to consider the capacity of senior centers to function as focal points. A number of observations lead to a negative assessment of this capacity. First, findings reviewed earlier indicate that senior centers serve the relatively healthy and well-off elderly. Second, while the breadth and depth of their programming varies considerably, many senior centers offer mostly socialization and recreational experiences along with some health education and preventive services. Third, many senior centers do not have the staff or physical facilities to plan or provide a wider range of services for frail or special need populations. Fourth, some observers argue that overall center utilization rates are too low to support focal point functions (Brown and O'Day, 1981). Finally, most senior centers are not centrally involved in comprehensive service planning and do not have the staff, resources, or organizational stature to be so involved.

The following observations can be made in rebuttal to these points. First, most senior centers by no means attract the healthiest, wealthiest, and most socially connected elderly; some serve elders with limited incomes, social contacts, and health. Second, the programming of senior centers can be seen as remarkably broad, given the resources made available to center staff. Third, providing services to special need populations requires skills and facilities that many senior centers do not possess. Yet some senior centers (albeit a minority) do provide services for the frail, such as adult daycare, or make less formal accommodations for center members who experience physical, mental, or social losses. Fourth, while it is true the majority of the elderly never attend a senior center, it is also true that more elderly utilize senior centers by far than any other community-based service. And fifth, federal legislation requires that Area Agencies on Aging perform comprehensive service planning, coordination, and provision. Both legally and practically, it is not the place of senior centers to perform that function.

Given the above, it would seem reasonable to conclude that senior centers do play important, but somewhat circumscribed, roles in the aging services network. They are not the ideal focal point for the elderly, but they can and do fulfill this function better than many other organizations. After all, how many elderly know what and where their local Area Agency on Aging is? Over the years, senior center programming has broadened, and centers' importance as delivery sites for many federally funded services has grown as well. It should be remembered that the medical and social service system in this country has become increasingly specialized. The nature and delivery mechanisms of services are largely driven by the regulations of funding agencies—be they private or public. Longterm community-based care in reality often means a number of discrete services for elderly with varying levels of health problems. The success and survival of senior centers, which usually are fashioned on a wellness, and nonmedical model—is actually quite remarkable. Clearly, however, not all senior centers are comprehensive, some do not even come close to the focal point ideal, and some are unlikely to be able or willing to perform this function.

SERVING THE FRAIL ELDERLY

One of the issues that is often (and increasingly) noted in regard to the role of senior centers in the continuum of services is how well they are able to meet the needs of the growing number of "old-old" and frail elderly. The frail elderly include persons with reduced physical and mental capabilities and diminished social support systems who need continuing assistance to maintain a household (Federal Council on Aging, 1978). Previous chapters have presented information relevant to these questions. Data on programming from a national sample of senior centers studied in the early 1980s by the author revealed only 12 percent reported offering adult daycare, 21 percent offered protective services, and 24 percent had programs for the handicapped. Sela (1986) found an even smaller percentage of a national sample offered activities directed to the hearing-impaired elderly. Other researchers have generally (but not always) found that senior center users have higher levels of health status than nonusers.

A number of studies of senior center participation and participants have observed that the frail elderly are undeserved by such places (Hanssen et al., 1978; Monk, 1988; Leanse and Wagener, 1975; Ralston, 1983). Other research suggests that relative to other organizations, senior centers are indeed significantly involved with programming for the frail (Jacobs, 1980; Kendon et al., 1988). Monk's (1988) in-depth study of senior centers and the frail elderly in New York state provides data that are of note. Almost 90 percent of the center directors in this sample claimed the frail were integrated into regular programming, and 21 percent said they developed separate programs for the frail. Overall, directors said that about 10 percent of their users were frail (mostly hearing, visual and mobility impairment), and one-half were not willing to increase that percentage. One-third of the center directors also indicated that the number of frail attending their center had increased in the last year.

There are, however, a number of arguments for why senior centers should work to include frail elders in their programming and why doing so may become increasingly necessary in the future. The first reason involves the federal legislative imperative of Section 504 of the 1973 Rehabilitation Act, which was implemented in 1977. This Act bars discrimination on the basis of handicaps, including hearing, vision, and mobility impairments, in all federally funded programs or services. Thus, any program receiving federal funds must accept qualified handicapped persons (Monk, 1988). Second, over the years, amendments to the Older Americans Act have increased the emphasis on targeting services to disadvantaged groups of elderly, including the frail. The 1987 amendments specifically noted that programs should address the needs of yet another special population—the developmentally disabled. It would appear that if senior centers do not respond to these priorities in a more formal manner, they may begin to experience a decline in program funding.

A third factor is the aging in place of current senior center populations. While hard data on this are sparse indeed, there is evidence to suggest that both the number and characteristics of senior center participants have changed significantly since the early 1980s. As noted in chapter five, telephone interviews with a random sample of over 100 rural Area Agency on Aging directors from across the country, carried out by the author as part of his national Area Agency on Aging study (Krout, 1989), provide empirical support for this hypothesis. Approximately 75 percent of these directors indicate that most, but not all, of the senior centers in their planning and service area have experienced a decline in attendance and difficulties in attracting the young-old or newly retired. This decline occurs when older center users die, move away, or cease participation due to serious health problems, and are not replaced by new and younger attenders in their sixties. One significant consequence has been that senior center populations overall are becoming older and more frail, a development that can precipitate a change in programming. Thus, senior centers may have no choice but to orient more programming to the frail if they want to avoid declines in participation.

Fourth, as discussed elsewhere in this chapter, senior center involvement in programming for the frail can be seen as an aspect of their focal point status. It can be argued that multipurpose, comprehensive senior centers, where resources permit, should reach out to serve elderly who are frail as well as those who are active. Involving the frail in senior centers will further their legitimacy. While the physical and financial resources available to senior centers may often not be as extensive as desired, they may be more extensive than can be found elsewhere. If the frail are to be integrated with the well, where else better to do this than in senior centers?

The fifth factor involves another imperative—a demographic one. Between 1980 and 1990, the number of elderly (sixty-five and older) in this nation is projected to increase 23 percent, from 25.5 million to 31.7 million. But the oldest-old, those eighty-five years of age and over and most likely to be frail, will grow much faster. This age group increased at double the rate of the elderly in general between 1980 and 1985; between 1985 and the year 2000, the old-old are expected to increase by 82 percent—four times the increase for the elderly overall (Soldo and Agree, 1988). These numbers of old-old will no doubt place burdens on many points of the longterm care system, and may well increase the need and demand for senior centers to accommodate frail elders in greater numbers and in a greater range of activities.

Finally, it should be noted that healthier senior center participants can be expected to learn from the frail. Up to this point, the underlying assumption in this discussion has been that involvement in senior center activities can help the frail. This implies that the benefits would be a one-way street going from the well to the frail, and suggest implicitly that the frail have little of value to offer others—that they are only takers, and not givers. It is suggested here that this is a narrow, even discriminatory, attitude. At the very least, well center participants could learn many things from the frail about different problems and how to cope with them. This information might well be useful as the well become more frail themselves.

Unfortunately, sufficient data are not available to determine current senior center involvement with the frail elderly. One of the problems is how to define "programming" or "involvement" with the frail. A senior center, especially a small one, may not offer specific programming for the frail, but may attempt to accommodate users with increasing levels of frailty. No efforts are made in this instance to recruit or integrate frail elderly who were not previously center participants. Whether or not this qualifies as serving the frail probably depends on one's perspective. Indeed, Monk's (1988) in-depth study of attitudes toward accommodation of the frail in New York state multipurpose senior centers found that both center staff and well users were more accepting of members who were already frail. The author's study of eight senior centers in western New York found that several of the centers quite successfully made provisions for the inclusion of mentally and physically impaired elderly in their activities. But the numbers of these elderly were very small, and their participation was limited to meals and a small number of programs (Krout, 1988).

Starting from the premise that attempts should be made to integrate more fully those frail elderly capable of benefiting from and being accommodated by senior centers, a number of questions arise. A fundamental issue is how well traditional well elderly participants can be mixed or integrated with the frail. For example, it could be argued that traditional users would resent attempts to accommodate significant numbers of mentally and physically impaired elderly in senior center activities. Such an attempt might alter the image of the center and lead to a decline in use by well elderly.

Monk's (1988) survey found that 80 percent of center directors felt their well users were accepting of the frail, but noted that frail elderly with mental impairment and behavioral problems would be less welcome. However, many center directors admitted during site visits that the well elderly were, in fact, reluctant to accept the frail. Both Monk (1988) and Jacobs (1980) report that center directors see their staff as very accepting of the frail. Clearly, particular effort must be paid to recognizing and responding to (with educational efforts) negative attitudes of well participants and staff.

But it is reasonable and important to ask how many frail seniors with different kinds of needs can be incorporated into senior centers with varying resource levels. From another perspective, the degree to which the at-risk or handicapped elderly actually would benefit from senior center participation is not known. For example, Muzzy (1982) reports that participants in adult daycare programs have serious reservations about involvement in a senior center. They fear they will not know people, will not fit in, or will be unable to participate given their health problems. However, a very slow and lengthy involvement process did seem to result in successful participation.

Another important issue is how well prepared, in general, senior centers are to accommodate the frail. Planning would appear to be essential in this regard. Monk (1988) reports that while four-fifths of the center directors in his sample said they were interested in increasing the number of frail participants, only one-quarter said they had actually implemented a specific program to do so. The need for greater planning for the frail elderly is noted by both Monk (1988) and Jacobs (1980). Lack of financial resources, space, and staff training are often cited as other barriers to senior center accommodation of the frail. For example, three-fifths of the directors in Monk's study reported needing increased funds to further the utilization of their centers by the frail. Center directors surveyed by Jacobs (1980) reported a similar concern, even though 40 percent said they received special funds to support programs for the frail. Lack of time is also seen by center directors as restricting their work with the frail.

In addition to money, staff training is critical if senior centers are to successfully incorporate increasing numbers of frail elderly into existing programs or develop special programs. Only about one-third to one-half of the center directors in Monk's (1988) study reported staff training in any of seven areas related to conditions of frailty, and almost 90 percent of the sample studied by Jacobs (1980) indicated a need for staff training in the needs of the frail. Often senior centers have only one or two full-time professional staff, and these people have multiple responsibilities. Ideally, additional monies would be made available to hire professional staff, but this is often not possible, and volunteers are relied on heavily for supervision or guidance of frail participants. How much and how well can volunteers be expected to do with the frail? Clearly, meaningful and effective involvement of the frail in senior centers requires in-depth training of volunteers and staff (Monk, 1988).

Several other points should be noted in regard to this issue. First, depending on their needs, frail elders require certain physical environmental supports. While Monk (1988) found that center directors in New York state felt their centers were generally well suited to accommodate the frail, this may well not be the case in other states. While integrating the frail into a center presumably means having them use the same facilities as well participants, this may not always be possible, and may require some changes in the center's physical environment. Not unrelated to the issue of space and its use is the issue of program integration. Recall that the large majority of center directors surveyed by Monk (1988) did not have programs for specific disabilities but reported that the frail were involved in regular center programming to varying degrees. It is not known to what extent and with what effect the frail attending senior centers are actually truly involved in general center programming. But as Monk (1988) observes, the frail elderly do have unique programming needs according to the level of their capabilities, and are not necessarily well-matched with all senior center activities.

Finally, it is clear that linkages with other agencies and organizations in the community are fundamental to the successful involvement of frail elders in senior centers. Two-thirds of the center directors surveyed by Jacobs (1980) noted that knowledge of community resources and information on successful programming models was a special need and 94 percent indicated that they coordinated services with other community agencies. For example, Hirsch (1977) discusses the slow and deliberative process by which nursing home patients were included in a senior center. Monk (1988) concludes that senior centers involving the frail elderly must utilize existing service networks for both diagnostic and programmatic resources. In addition, other services are often required to locate and provide access to potential participants.

This point raises an additional policy question. Assuming that senior centers can effectively bring frail elders into their activities, to what degree would this involve competition with organizations having the responsibility and expertise for serving the at-risk? In an ideal world, existing resources would be used to the greatest benefit of those in need, and not in response to ownership claims based on expertise or professional turf. In the real world, however, frail elders can represent valuable sources of income for various agencies in need of clients to justify their existence and pay their bills. Yet community resources for the frail are, and are likely to remain, woefully inadequate; existing resources must be utilized where available. Frail elderly should be encouraged to participate in and be accommodated by other community-based services, where appropriate. To imply that frail elderly should only be assisted by in-home services or in institutions feeds off the dichotomy of well versus frail elderly services that is often criticized in theory. The idea that services for one can and should not be mixed with services for the other may do a disservice to both the frail and well and result in an underutilization of resources that could significantly improve the quality of life and functioning of many frail elders.

IMPACT AND EFFECTIVENESS

Most of this book has considered what senior centers are, what they do, how much they do, and for whom. Another important question concerns the quality of senior center programming and its impact on center participants. Despite the centrality of these questions for an assessment of senior centers and policy issues, few studies have attempted to conceptualize, let alone measure, the quality and impact of senior center programming. This issue can be viewed from two per-spectives—the center participant and the aging services network in general. From the participant perspective, the question is how senior center attendance affects their daily lives, socialization, health, and so forth. Previous chapters have presented theories concerning the benefits of senior center attendance. These include education, socialization, health, self-enhancement, friendship and con-fidant relationships, community involvement, and information on or linkage with a wide range of community services. And it has been suggested that senior centers might especially be beneficial for rural elderly, who have limited alter-natives for social interaction and who generally live in communities with fewer services (Krout, 1986; Ralston, 1983).

However, there are almost no data that measure these supposed benefits. Data showing that senior center users report better health and higher levels of social interaction and life satisfaction than nonusers do not prove that senior center attendance, per se, is the cause of these advantages. Few studies have reported findings on the impact of center attendance from the participant's perspective. Indeed, an intensive review of the senior center literature by Ralston (1987, 208) concludes that "there is almost no empirical research documenting the quality of activities and services in senior centers." From a somewhat broader per-spective, the question is the actual effectiveness of center programming in meet-ing different needs of the elderly living in the community.

Turning first to the question of program effectiveness, it should be noted that several gerontological observers have expressed reservations about senior centers. Matthews (1979) argues that senior centers promote a social image of old age that is based on incompetence; it has also been said that senior centers serve to intensify the age-segregated nature of America's aging policy and of American society in general. The small number of studies that have focused on the qualitative aspects of senior center programming have not been very positive in their conclusions. Most of these studies have focused on the effectiveness of education programs. For example, Jones (1976) concluded that educational activities received a much lower priority than social programs in five Rhode Island senior centers. Jacobs' (1982) conclusion that educational goals are not a high priority among senior staff, board members, or participants is also noted by Meredith and Aimor (1976). Ralston (1981) reports that most of the five centers in her study did not provide adequate programming in areas such as personal development, problems of aging, and home and family.

Guttmann and Miller (1972) studied the provision of health, financial, housing, and employment services for a nationwide sample of seventy senior centers, and concluded that they were significantly inadequate. Daum and Dobrof (1983) found that senior centers in New York were much more capable of meeting some of their participants' needs than others elsewhere. They report that the colder winter weather in New York state brought an increase in demand for services such as transportation, energy assistance, in-home meals, telephone reassurance, friendly visits, and escorts. However, the senior centers were best prepared to provide congregate meals and recreation. Finally, the findings of one of the only studies designed to uncover the impact of senior center participation through longitudinal data could be termed disappointing. Schneider et al. (1985) collected information from 500 rural Arkansas elders both at the start and after two years of participation in a senior center, and compared them with a sample of non-attenders. They reported that senior center programs tended to reach socially active elderly who were not high risks for institutionalization, and that center participation did not appear to lower rates of institutionalization, improve health and life outlook, or increase utilization rates of other government programs.

Nonetheless, with the exception of Schneider et al. (1985), these studies question either the basic concept or programming capability of senior centers. It is clear that there is great variability in the breadth and depth of senior center programming in the United States. But it should be noted that finding senior centers do not offer enough programming in certain areas does not speak to the issue of how the programming they do conduct affects participants, or how attendance at a senior center may benefit an older person in a general sense. Several studies have attempted to determine this, at least from the elderly participant's perspective.

Hanssen et al. (1978) report that senior center participants had few complaints about the services they received. Poll (1975), in a study of two Chicago senior centers, found that 94 percent of the staff and membership at each center said that the members were satisfied with their participation, and that half of the attenders viewed interpersonal relationships as the main source of this satisfaction. Finally, the author's recent in-depth study of participation in eight western New York senior centers provides some detailed data on the impact of centers from the elder's perspective (Krout, 1988). Since so little information is available on this topic, findings from this study will be presented in some detail.

Data on the impact of senior center attendance were collected from a random sample of over 200 users of eight senior centers. Study participants were asked to respond to ten statements about "coming to this center." All of the statements were positive. Ninety percent or more of the elderly strongly agreed or agreed that the center helped them keep healthy, active, make new friends, improve their social life, and feel better about themselves. Almost 80 percent said it helped them learn new things, and three-quarters said it made them feel more self-confident. Seventy percent agreed or strongly agreed that going to the center made them feel more independent, and three-fifths indicated it helped them eat better. Only 40 percent agreed that center participation helped them manage their money better. A summed impact score was computed by assigning a one for each statement a person strongly agreed or agreed with. Surprisingly, no socio-demographic variables were found to be significantly related to this score. Participants were also asked how their lives would change if they did not attend a senior center. Eighteen percent indicated that they would be more lonely and would have to find something else to do. One in six of the respondents said life would be more boring, and 14 percent said they would not get out as much.

The author's data come from a small and geographically restricted sample and refer only to participant perceptions of the effectiveness and impact of senior centers. It is clear that there is a dearth of research on these important issues. Such data are needed not only to determine the role played by centers in the aging services network, but also to assist center operators evaluate center philosophy and programming.

USE OF RESOURCES

A final issue in need of attention is one of resources. Do society or the elderly get their money's worth from senior centers? Could the resources that go to senior centers be better used to serve different needs or segments of the older population? Should senior centers be doing more? Obviously, these are not simple questions, and the answers depend significantly on assumptions about many things. First, it should be noted that senior centers provide quite a bit of service for relatively little money. Few senior centers make profits, and data in chapter three showed that employment as a senior center director or program coordinator is hardly a route to riches. Senior centers make extensive use of volunteers and generally have low overhead, with most of the dollars going into essential areas or programming. Indeed, given their resources, it is often remarkable they are able to do what they do. Could senior centers do more? Yes, many could with additional resources for staff and staff training, facilities, and access. But, is it fair or reasonable to state that senior centers don't do enough, given their resource situations? Businesses are not expected to make and sell products if they do not have the resources.

The more fundamental issue really is what they do and for whom. In this era of decreasing resources and increasing numbers of frail home-bound elderly, can the nation afford the luxury of senior centers? Perhaps the more appropriate question is, should government use scarce revenues for senior centers? Few people would deny the right of older people to pay for all of the costs associated with programs at their senior centers. At the core, this is really a question about the basic philosophy behind the Older Americans Act of supporting services for the elderly that are not means-tested (sliding contribution scales are allowed) and are not directed to the sickest, most needy elderly in society. It certainly would appear that increasingly tough resource choices will have to be made at the federal, state, and local levels, and that some social, recreational, and even nutritional programs will face reduced public funding.

But a very fine line must be tread here. It is easy to measure the cost of senior center programs, but much more difficult to measure their benefit. How does one qualify the benefits of focal point activities and socialization experiences? Means-testing programs would likely turn a senior center into just another welfare program in the eyes of many elderly and might well lead many participants to drop out. A significant withdrawal of public funding, or redirection of senior center programs to more frail populations, would change the nature of senior centers. It is by no means certain that the large majority of more healthy attenders who might drop out would find other sources from which to get the benefits they currently get from senior centers. It is doubtful that senior centers could continue to play focal point roles in this situation.

Given these observations, some would argue that the appropriate question should be can we afford not to continue public support of senior centers? As has been noted, many senior centers are currently undergoing changes in their user populations that are a result of larger demographic, social, and economic trends, as well as changes in funding or programming emphasis. Senior center populations are getting older and more frail through an aging in-place of users and through an inability to attract increasingly healthy and wealthy, newly retired people in their sixties. This change puts the question of whether society should pay in a somewhat different light. Indeed, the argument could, and surely will, be made that the public commitment to senior centers should increase as their user population changes. More problematic is a decline in the numbers of senior center attenders should it become large. A trend toward significantly lower numbers might well affect the bottom-line cost per unit of service measures, as well as the political attractiveness of and justification for senior centers.

Unfortunately, policymakers have not generated a united strategy for addressing the needs of the elderly nor have goals and objectives for senior centers been unambiguously stated. Much of the data needed to determine whether senior centers are the best use of available resources is lacking. In the absence of clear goals and good data—and often, even when they are available—resource allocation decisions are based on bits and pieces of information, opinions, and political considerations. There is little data to prove that senior centers do a bad job, and some data to suggest they do a good job. Many senior centers also have built strong local bases of support. It would appear, then, that a serious direct challenge to the appropriateness of senior centers and their activities is unlikely, but that broader demographic and social changes, as well as changes in levels and emphasis of health and social service funding, may well require changes in center focus.

RESEARCH QUESTIONS

A broad range of questions has been raised throughout this chapter that point the way for future investigations and analyses. The basic thrust of this chapter has been to examine where senior centers fit into the aging services network. One important issue in this regard is the role senior centers play as focal points. However, while the author has suggested a number of arguments that support the view of senior centers as focal points, the fact remains that there is a paucity of research on this issue. This is perhaps understandable, since the focal point concept itself has not been clearly defined. There are no data that show the degree to which senior centers actually carry out focal point functions, or that measure the impact of such activities on the elderly or on other organizations in the aging services network. The resources (staff, facilities, and so on) necessary to effectively carry out focal point activities, and the circumstances under which such activities are appropriate, have not been clearly identified. The nature and importance of senior centers taking focal point roles in rural versus urban areas, or in different regions of the country, have not been explored. And what of the future? How central will, or should, the focal point concept be to senior centers in the next ten to twenty years?

A large number of questions have been raised regarding the desirability and capability of senior centers integrating frail elders into their facilities and programming. Clearly, more research needs to be conducted on these issues, as well as on the current level of senior center activity with the frail. Precious little data are available on the number of elders with different physical and psychological deficits now served by senior centers, types of center programming made available to them, and the impact of such programming on the frail. The consequences of the involvement of frail elders on other participants and the center as a whole are also not known. Other questions in need of research concern the types of resources, planning, training, and programming necessary to accommodate successfully various levels and types of frail individuals. In short, what works and why? How can new members who first enter the center after they have become frail best be accommodated? The desirability, necessity, and impact of increasing the numbers of frail elderly in senior centers in the future must also be examined.

In addition, it is clear that very little information is available on the impact or effectiveness of senior centers. Researchers have been so busy collecting data on who uses senior centers that they have neglected to find out what happens to people once they become involved. To what degree and in what ways does senior center participation benefit the elderly? The data to answer this question are largely anecdotal, or involve participant perceptions. The question of impact and effectiveness can also be asked from a broader perspective. Could or should the resources put into senior centers be better spent elsewhere to benefit the elderly? Few researchers have questioned the costs versus the benefits of senior centers from this broader policy stance.

CHAPTER SUMMARY

This chapter has explored several policy-related aspects of senior centers. The role played by senior centers as focal points in the aging services network has been considered. It is evident that many senior centers are called upon to fulfull this role, and the author would argue that the rationales for using senior centers in this manner outweigh the reasons not to. However, few data are available to examine questions related to senior center focal point activities, and it is clear that not all senior centers are equipped to handle such responsibilities. The focal point issue provides numerous research opportunities that strike at the heart of the question of what senior centers do and what they can contribute to the larger service network as service providers, service delivery sites, and referral/outreach organizations.

Another fundamental issue examined in this chapter relates to the type of programming offered and participants served by senior centers—specifically, involvement with frail or at-risk elderly. Senior centers have been criticized by some for not being able or willing to involve significant numbers of the frail in center programming. Again, there is a great need for research in this area. The few studies that have been conducted suggest that most senior centers accommodate small numbers of frail elderly. However, as senior center directors have appropriately noted in several research projects, integrating the frail successfully requires money, for staffing, facilities, participant education, special transportation, and so forth. The author has observed that senior centers should not be expected dramatically to increase their work with the frail without a concomitant increase in resources. While senior centers should and will (as their users age in place) pay more attention to meeting the needs of the frail, it would not be appropriate to require them to focus solely on the frail. Much needs to be learned about how to most effectively mix the frail with healthier center populations.

A third issue receiving attention in this chapter underlies much of the literature on senior centers—their effectiveness and impact. Some authors have argued that senior center programming is limited or ineffective, and serves populations that really do not have levels of need justifying the public and private resources expended on them. The author suggests caution in making such judgements.

Very little, if any, research has been carried out that directly measures the impact of senior center activities on the individual or on the broader aging services network. Costs and benefits are extremely difficult to measure, and are usually interpreted differently depending on one's assumptions, values, and ideology. The small amount of existing research suggests that senior center participants are indeed satisfied with and see benefits from their center involvement. But larger questions do remain concerning the most appropriate use of the resources that go into senior centers. Fundamentally, these are questions about the goals and regulations of the Older Americans Act, and about the configuration of community-based services for the elderly.

REFERENCES

Binner, P. (1986). *DRG's and the administration of mental health services*. Englewood Cliffs, NJ: Prentice-Hall.

Brown, C., & O'Day, M. (1981). Services to the elderly. In N. Gilbert and H. Specht (Eds.), *Handbook of Social Services*. Englewood Cliffs, NJ: Prentice-Hall.

Daum, M., & Dobrof, R. (1983). Seasonal vulnerability of the old and the cold: The role of the senior citizens center. *Journal of Gerontological Social Work, 5*, 81–106.

Federal Council on Aging. (1978). Public policy and the frail elderly. Washington, DC: U.S. Department of Health, Education and Welfare.

Guttmann, D., & Miller, P. (1972). Perspectives on the provision of social services in senior centers. *The Gerontologist, 12*, 403–406.

Hanssen, A., Meima, N., Buckspan, L., Henderson, B., Helbig, T., & Zarit, S. (1978). Correlates of senior center participation. *The Gerontologist, 18*, 193–199.

Hirsch, C. (1977). Integrating the nursing home resident into a senior citizens center. *The Gerontologist, 17*, 277–234.

Jacobs, B. (1980). Senior centers and the at-risk older person. Washington, DC: The National Council on the Aging.

Jacobs, B. (1982). Educational goals for senior centers: A study of perceptions of reality and aspirations. *Dissertation Abstracts International, 42*, 4253-A.

Jones, E. (1976). An analysis of adult education programs in selected senior citizen centers in Rhode Island. *Dissertation Abstracts International, 37*, 5529-A.

Kendon, J., Hughes, S., Campione, P., & Goldberg, R. (1988). Shedding new light on adult day care. *Perspective on Aging*, November/December, 18–21.

Krout, J. (1986). *The aged in rural America*. Westport, CT: Greenwood Press.

Krout, J. (1987). Senior center linkages and the provision of services to the elderly. Final report to the AARP Andrus Foundation. Fredonia, New York.

Krout, J. (1988). The frequency, duration, stability, and discontinuation of senior center participation: Causes and consequences. Final report to the AARP Andrus Foundation. Fredonia, New York.

Krout, J. (1989). Area agencies on aging: Service provision and planning for the rural elderly. Final report to the Retirement Research Foundation. Fredonia, New York.

Leanse, J. (1977). The senior center, individuals and the community. In R. Kadish (Ed.), *The later years: Social applications of gerontology*. Belmont, CA: Brooks/Cole.

Leanse, J., & Wagener, L. (1975). Senior centers: A report of senior group programs in America. Washington, DC: National Council on the Aging.

Matthews, S. (1979). *The social world of old women: Management of self-identity.* Newbury Park, CA: Sage.

Meredith, G., & Aimor, C. (1976). Indexing the polarization of social groups in a multipurpose senior center. *Psychological Reports, 39,* 88–90.

Monk, A. (1988). The integration of frail elderly into senior centers. Final report to the AARP Andrus Foundation. Columbia University, New York.

Muzzy, C. (1982). Senior centers: Linking the impaired to the community. *Perspective on Aging.* July/August, 22–23.

National Association of State Units on Aging. (1983). A profile of state and area agencies on aging. Washington, DC.

Poll, S. (1975). The challenge of older adult's satisfaction with participation in a community center. Senior centers: Realizing our potential. Proceedings of the Eighth National Conference of Senior Centers, September 1973, Chicago.

Ralston, P. (1981). Educational needs and activities of older adults: Their relationship to senior center programs. *Educational Gerontology, 7,* 231–244.

Ralston, P. (1983). Senior centers in rural communities: A qualitative study. Paper presented at the annual meeting of the Gerontological Society of America, San Francisco.

Ralston, P. (1987). Senior center research: Policy from knowledge? In E. Borgatta and R. Montgomery (Eds.), *Critical issues in aging policy: Linking research and values.* Newbury Park, CA: Sage.

Schneider, M., Chapman, D., & Voth, D. (1985). Senior center participation: A two-stage approach to impact evaluation. *The Gerontologist, 25,* 194–200.

Sela, I. (1986). A study of programs and services for the hearing impaired elderly in senior centers and clubs in the U.S. Unpublished dissertation. Washington, DC: Gallaudet College.

Soldo, B., & Agree, E. (1988). America's elderly. *Population Bulletin, 43,* 3, September.

U.S. Department of Health and Human Services (1988). Final regulations, Older Americans Act: Grants for State and Community Programs on Aging. Washington, DC: U.S.G.P.O.

Wagener, L. (1981). The concept of a focal point for service delivery in the field of aging: Washington, DC: National Council on the Aging.

Weber, M. (1947). *The theory of social and economic organization.* New York: Free Press.

Weiss, T. (1986). A legislative view of Medicare and DRG's. *American Psychologist, 41,* 79–82.

9

Summary and Conclusions

THE ROAD TRAVELED

This book has attempted a comprehensive examination of senior centers in the United States. It began with a consideration of how senior centers can be defined, and much of the remainder of the book has explored, at least implicitly, the various components of that definition. The nature of what senior centers are and what they do has required that this examination be multifaceted and multilevel. The predominant senior center research focus has traditionally been on programming efforts and client populations. These important issues have been explored, but a fuller understanding of senior centers requires a consideration of their organizational characteristics and resources, their historical growth and development, the roles they play in the larger community-based service system for the elderly, and the ways in which national aging legislation (particularly the Older Americans Act) has both affected and reflected what senior centers are and what they do. This book has attempted to pull together the existing research on various aspects of senior centers to further this understanding. Thus, a consideration of senior center programming is relevant not only to questions of impact on participants, but also to the role senior centers play in the service system.

To use an analogy, this book has tried to put together a senior center puzzle that is connected to other social service puzzles. Quite a bit of information on senior centers has been uncovered, but it has also become evident that quite a few of the pieces are missing or incomplete. The author has laid claim to the importance of and need for attempts to solve this puzzle. Hopefully, the validity of these claims has been well documented, even if the senior center puzzle is not perfect. That is, not all the pieces fit just right, some may be missing, and the placement of some pieces can be disputed. Important questions do exist concerning how well senior centers work, what they do and who they affect, as well as their past, present, and future roles in relation to larger policy needs and agendas. This was clearly noted as one of the author's assumptions or starting points.

Two other characteristics of this puzzle should be noted before proceeding. The first is that the puzzle is a generic one. It does not apply to all senior centers. Indeed, one of the other points of departure noted in the first chapter was that a rich and complex diversity characterizes many aspects of senior centers in the United States today. The author has tried to illustrate and document this variation while building a generalized overview of senior centers. A second characteristic is that the puzzle presented here is, to a large degree, suspended in time. An attempt has been made to provide the reader with a historical perspective on senior centers, and to note change where the data permits; the last section of this chapter explores the future of senior centers. But, the senior center dynamic or process—the ebb and flow of the movement—has not been particularly well captured. This observation leads to a consideration of some of the other roads this book has not traveled.

All books take on the theoretical and methodological orientations of their authors. Since this book has attempted to integrate the existing senior center research, it has also reflected the approaches that other researchers have taken in their studies. By and large, this approach has been descriptive and functional. Little if any work, including the author's, has considered senior centers from a conflict or symbolic interactionist perspective. Specific substantive research questions in need of further examination are reviewed later in this chapter. But there is larger research need here, the need for academics to view senior centers through other analytical frameworks. An understanding of the meaning and importance of senior centers for participants, as well as many aspects of senior center dynamics, can clearly be increased through an interactionist perspective. A deeper appreciation of center linkages and of the place of centers in aging policy at the local, state, and national level can be gained through a conflict perspective. The information produced by such viewpoints would be of use to practitioners as well as academic researchers.

Finally, an important source of information about senior centers has largely been untapped. This is the knowledge and experience of the hundreds of persons who have helped establish and build individual senior centers across this country. While center directors are often asked by researchers to fill out mail surveys, and sometimes participate in in-person interviews, the published literature reveals few attempts to utilize these and other knowledgeable local resources. Hopefully, this drawback will also be corrected by future students of senior centers.

OVERVIEW OF MAJOR FINDINGS

Various definitions suggest that a number of common characteristics identify senior centers in general. These include: serving the elderly; occupying a designated physical place; providing a broad range of activities and services; development from a community planning process; working with other organizations; acting as a visible focal point; and providing opportunities to the elderly for community involvement, social interaction, friendship, and personal growth. Senior centers across the nation exhibit considerable variation as to the degree and way in which they display these characteristics. A certain amount of definitional imprecision then, is probably unavoidable and perhaps even desirable in considerations of senior centers. Because of the wide range of variation found between senior centers, existing models do not adequately capture what senior centers in fact are. For example, while Taietz's (1976) distinction between the ''voluntary organization'' versus ''social agency'' nature of senior centers is useful, the reality is much more complex.

Most senior centers have been in existence for less than two decades, and their growth and development is rooted in both local and national factors. Indeed, it is difficult to separate these two. The large majority of senior centers emerged in the 1970s when federal recognition and support for the senior center concept emerged in the form of amendments to the Older Americans Act. This support included both funding to local areas for center development and the identification of multipurpose senior centers as focal points for services to the elderly. Data suggest that the number of senior centers has grown from approximately 1,000 in 1970 to approximately 10,000 today. Several other national developments played significant a role in the evolution of senior centers—the White House Conferences on Aging and the growth of a national senior center interest group, the National Institute of Senior Centers of the National Council on the Aging.

Many of the organizational characteristics of senior centers appear to have changed over the past two decades, partly due to the increased resources and recognition they received in the 1970s. Most senior centers are defined as multipurpose, as subunits of other organizations, and are located in separate facilities. Their budgets are relatively small and come from a broad range of sources. Thus, while federal monies are probably the biggest single source of center and center programming support, they appear to account for less than one-third of center funding in general. State and local governments, as well as participant contributions, are also important funding sources. Senior centers also have few paid staff and rely heavily on volunteers, usually participants. Center directors are considerably more educated and thus more professional than they were even a decade ago, but still receive relatively low salaries. Finally, the goals center directors identify relate largely to providing services and increasing the elderly's independence and quality of life. Thus, the underlying goals of senior centers would appear in general to be oriented toward improving or maintaining the lives of their participants—an internal focus—rather than toward focal point or linkage roles—an external focus.

Increased resources appear to have led to an increase in the depth and breadth of senior center programming over the years. Yet most centers are still more likely to offer certain activities and services than others. For example, a considerably higher percentage of centers report programming in areas such as access to center, health and nutrition, information and assistance, education, recreation, and volunteer opportunities. Programming involving services such as counseling, income supplement, in-home, and special services for the frail or disabled is not widespread. Indeed, programming for such special populations is generally viewed as inadequate; this is a fundamental issue for senior center philosophy and operation. The overall quantity of center offerings has been found to be moderately related to center resources and participant characteristics.

Perhaps because of this varied programming, national data indicate that from 15 to 20 percent of the elderly attend a senior center and/or eat a meal there at least once a year; local studies suggest the vast majority of center users attend their center at least once a week. Thus, centers are by far the most often utilized community service for the elderly, even though attendance rates vary considerably from place to place. Senior centers have almost universal recognition among the elderly, but knowledge about specific programming and operation is quite limited. In addition, most elderly have either positive or at worst neutral attitudes toward senior centers. The information seniors do have about centers is gained from a variety of sources, with nonusers receiving information largely from informal networks.

Lack of a general awareness of senior centers would not appear to account for why many elderly do not attend them. Existing research suggests that the elderly who use senior centers do so because they enjoy the activities and the opportunities for the social interaction and companionship. Seniors who do not participate in centers appear to do so because they are either too busy or not interested, or because they or their spouse are in poor health. The considerable amount of research attention paid to comparing users and nonusers has yielded a potpourri of findings. The most consistent finding has been that users are healthier and have higher levels of life satisfaction and social contact than nonusers, although the causal relationship between these variables and center participation has not been carefully investigated. Overall, the work on correlates of center utilization suffers because researchers do not conceptualize this variable as a continuum ranging from nonuse to former use.

This book has also documented that the majority of senior centers engage in working relationships or linkages with a wide variety of other organizations in their efforts to meet the needs of the elderly. The most prevalent and preferred type of linkage is informal in nature and involves referral exchanges with other organizations. The nature of the linkage differs, however, according to the type of service involved. A number of barriers, most notably lack of time, funding, or staff, do inhibit linkage activity. Nonetheless, center directors indicate that the number of organizations they work with has increased recently, and will either increase or remain stable in the near future. These linkages expand the capability of senior centers to bring services to the elderly and heighten the role senior centers play as focal points in the community.

Finally, virtually all of the topics examined in this book are relevant to larger policy questions about the impact and importance of senior centers as a mechanism for meeting the needs of various segments of the elderly population, and about the contributions senior centers make to the community-based aging services network. The information just reviewed on linkages is central to the consideration of senior center focal point activities. Although not well-defined, this term implies a central and highly visible role as a delivery site for services and information or referrals for aging services in the community. Senior centers, generally speaking, appear to be good focal point candidates, but their effectiveness in this role has not been empirically demonstrated. Another important policy question is the role that senior centers play in meeting the needs of the frail elderly. While there is some debate on this point, it would appear that the vast majority of senior center programming is not oriented to the frail, nor are senior centers generally prepared to strike out in this direction, even though their membership is getting older. Debates about the appropriateness, likelihood, or necessity of such moves aside, it is clear that a significant shift toward programming for the frail will require considerable planning, education, and resources.

The impact and effectiveness of senior centers both in regard to individual center participants and as a component of the overall aging services network constitutes a policy question that underlies all others. The meager amount of available research shows that center participants enjoy attending their senior center and feel they reap significant benefits from their involvement. It is also evident that senior centers make important contributions to the overall aging services network. Yet when issues concerning basic resource allocation, equity, and effectiveness or impact of the aging system are raised, some important and fundamental questions remain about the nature and activities of senior centers.

WHAT NEEDS TO BE LEARNED

One of the rationales given for writing this book was that a dearth of information exists on senior centers. A large number of issues in need of further consideration and research have been identified in the previous chapters. It may be useful to provide an overview of these major questions as this exploration of the senior center puzzle draws to a close.

Perhaps the most fundamental deficiency in the literature is an absence of work at the conceptual and theoretical level. This deficiency exists in examinations of center programming, awareness, utilization, participation, linkages, and so on. The lack of conceptual frameworks compounds the difficulties inherent in integrating research findings from various studies and limits the conclusions that can be drawn for both research and policy issues. The great variation between senior centers only increases the need for this work. Agreement on the essential components of a definition of senior centers is a first step in the conceptual arena.

A second fundamental set of questions relates to the broader historical and

social forces that have shaped and continue to shape the development and activities of senior centers. The author has attempted to outline some of these in
chapter two, but there is much to be learned. These factors operate at the national
and local levels and both need to be investigated. The same can be said for
another fundamental question—how and why do senior centers work? Almost
no attention has been paid to the micro- and macro-processes that shape senior
centers on a daily basis. The interpersonal and inter/intraorganizational dynamics
behind center programming, participation, and linkages are rarely explored. In
addition, the nature and impact of center facilities, staff, and budgets are rarely
brought into the research picture. The relatively small amount of information
presented on these aspects here will hopefully be relevant to further investigations
of these processes.

Ironically, even those topics on which researchers have focused are not really
well understood. Most of the data on programming, for example, relate to its
quantity, not its content, quality, or impact. Little is understood about the variables responsible for differences in these programming characteristics. The same
observation applies to senior center participants and participation. The relative
importance of the various factors that determine whether or not and to what
degree elders participate in centers has not been uncovered. The vast majority
of studies rely on a simple dichotomy of use versus nonuse, and ignore the
broader continuum of participation.

Finally, the role senior centers play in the larger community-based service
system for the elderly has been sorely neglected. The author has attempted to
shed some light on this question through a presentation of data on linkages and
a consideration of the focal point concept. But this work can stand only as a
first step. Again the process, benefits, cost, difficulties, and so forth of such
linkages should be investigated in much greater detail. Where researchers have
asked questions relevant to the roles played by senior centers, they have tended
to focus on narrow issues such as programming for the frail. This is an important
issue, but it should be evaluated in regard to broader policy matters not simply
the narrow question of what groups senior centers serve.

The research questions reviewed above focus on what senior centers are and
do, how they do it, and how they affect the elderly. Another set of issues revolves
around the question of what senior centers should be doing. These issues or
concerns are really policy issues, and are often formulated in the absence or
neglect of adequate and appropriate research findings. A number of important
policy issues regarding senior centers have been noted in this book. Most of
these issues revolve around the programming and participant mix of senior
centers, but some strike at the very heart of the senior center concept. Listed
below are a number of policy questions that are important from the author's
perspective and that probably will become more important in the not too distant
future.

—Who should senior centers serve?

—What emphasis should be placed on programming for the frail and needy versus the well elderly?

—Do senior centers have significant and positive impact on their users?

—Should centers focus more on services and less on recreation and socialization?

—Should linkages and focal point activities be given more importance?

—Where should resources for center operation and programming come from?

—Should center staff be required to be more professional?

—Are senior centers the most effective use of the resources currently put into them?

—Do senior centers further the degree of age segregation in society?

—What form and function should senior centers have in the future?

These are not simple questions and they do not have simple answers. The diversity of senior centers makes their assessment all the more difficult. The posing of these questions should not be interpreted necessarily as a criticism of senior centers as they are found in America today. Indeed, one response to these questions is no response. Senior centers are doing just fine, thank you, and any fundamental tampering with their basic structure, roles, or programming would be counterproductive. Significant changes in functions would require significant increases in resources. Policy makers should not forget that, measured by many yardsticks, senior centers have been very successful. And senior center practitioners have themselves examined questions such as these over the years in an effort to be more effective and responsive. Nevertheless, questions such as those noted above should and no doubt will be asked, and it is quite possible that future social, economic, and demographic trends will lead senior centers in somewhat different directions than those from which they have come. The following section considers the challenges senior centers are likely to face in the future.

LOOKING TOWARD THE FUTURE

It has been noted in several places in this book that the last several years have witnessed a leveling off and even a decline in senior center attendance in many areas around the country, and that senior centers are increasingly unable to attract newly retired, young-old participants. These trends threaten the very future of senior center viability, and could diminish their centrality as focal points in the aging services system. Precious little data on these changes have surfaced, and there is a great need for research on current projected patterns of senior center utilization. A decline in demand for programs housed in most senior centers (such as congregate meals) would probably result in decreased funding unless other programming emphases were increased. Such a decline in demand could not come at a more critical time. The 1980s has been a decade of decreased federal aid to many social services and to state and local governments. Given the enormity of the federal deficit, local governments will increasingly have to go it alone, and service agencies such as senior centers will have to rely more and more on participant contributions and fund-raising for dollars.

Indeed, these are only two of the conclusions of a national study of the impact of federal policies on nonprofit organizations serving the elderly, conducted between 1981 and 1984 (Wood et al., 1985). This study also reports "greater polarization between centers serving the poor and centers serving the nonpoor, more vigorous attempts to increase program income and an awareness of more fiscal austerity to come" (Wood, 1985). Reductions in federal resources were reported to result in cutbacks in staff, a shift from multiple to single-service specialization, and increased targeting to in-home services for the frail. Wood (1985) sees this as leading to a breakdown in the care coordination capabilities of the service network in general, and increased restriction in the range of services provided by agencies with a largely poor clientele. There is little reason to expect such trends have recently changed or are likely to do so in the near future.

Will senior centers survive into the twenty-first century? Most likely the simple answer to that question is yes. But how well and in what form? Changes in participant characteristics often bring changes in the activities of organizations. Senior centers may well be caught in a particularly challenging dilemma—how can programming be oriented to attract younger new members, even as current users grow older?

The larger policy issue for the center system and individual senior centers alike is: what should senior centers be in the future, and how can they get there? Such questions are difficult enough to formulate and consider in good economic times, but resource exigencies make them almost impossible to respond to effectively and appropriately. Perhaps the most regretful aspect of precipitious cutbacks in funding is that they generally force sudden change without planning. It would indeed be unfortunate if wholesale changes come to senior centers in the next decade simply because money becomes scarcer—although this would not be a particularly unusual occurrence in the United States.

It would be incorrect to state that senior centers are not in need of change. Many center practitioners are constantly searching for new roles and new approaches to serving the elderly, and are themselves pushing for change; some are not. Unfortunately, the environment in which senior centers and other parts of the aging services network operate is extremely complex. The impact of policy changes on the demand for and support of services is rarely well-documented, less well-understood, and never adequately anticipated. This notwithstanding, now is the time to formulate the debate, and to collect the information, on the desirability and impact of alternative senior center futures. The framers of this debate would be well-advised to recognize that much of the strength—and some of the weakness—of senior centers comes from their considerable diversity, and that this diversity requires that policy discussions allow for variation in senior centers in the future as well.

The reader may be disappointed that the author has not provided an in-depth answer to the question posed on the previous page: What should senior centers be and do in the future? An answer to that question is contingent on many unknowns—resource availability, health and social policy emphases, retirement and labor force trends, and so on. Nonetheless, some points can be made concerning the future of senior centers that will hopefully serve as a starting point.

One point is that demographic trends in the next twenty years may actually help buy some time for those pondering this question. The overall number of elderly is projected to grow modestly in the next two decades—between 10 and 12 percent—because of low depression-era fertility levels. However, the number of ''old-old'' will increase much more rapidly (Soldo and Agree, 1988). Indeed, the aging of the current center user population is part of this trend. Senior center populations are likely to get older regardless of the center's ability to attract new participants. Thus, senior centers must begin to plan for this eventuality now. This involves not only questions of programming for increasingly frail center users, but also programming that will be of interest to the young-old over a span of some twenty years.

Senior centers should continue to expand and diversify programming to meet the needs and interests of the elderly with different capabilities and interests, and to do so from a life-long learning perspective. Centers that simply provide a noon meal, recreation/socialization, and monthly health/education ''specials'' are not likely, in the author's opinion, to prosper in the future. Some centers might successfully follow the lead of the AARP and provide a large array of membership benefits, activities, and challenges. Other centers will not find such an approach feasible or desirable. Senior centers must attract the interest of the young-old or newly retired, but not abandon the growing number of elderly who survive into their eighties with most of their physical and mental facilities intact.

It is also likely that senior centers will, by necessity and choice, become both more interdependent and independent. The continued success of senior centers will require a strengthening and broadening of the linkage and focal point roles they currently play. Increased partnerships with the health, education, and business sectors of society will be a central part of this process. Most senior centers currently do not take advantage of the educational resources in their communities, nor do they contribute their own educational resources to their communities. The business sector has increasingly responded to the elderly as a market segment in recent years, and it is beginning to realize the importance of seniors as a resource.

Senior centers also represent a potential delivery site for health services beyond education and blood-pressure screening. Senior centers must expand their involvement in these areas and become more than focal points within the traditional aging services network. This will involve risks to be sure, but senior centers have taken similar risks in the past and prospered. By becoming involved in more aspects of community and society, senior centers will expand their resources and actually be able to become more independent. They will come to depend less on monies from aging programs that are likely to shrink in the future.

Another aspect of this interdependence involves a greater partnership with organizations representing other groups. The elderly are increasingly portrayed in society as selfish, and as getting more than their fair share of resources. Regardless of the truth of this image, it is likely to grow in the future. Thus, it is both politically expedient and morally appropriate for senior centers to become more responsive to the needs of other groups in society. There is much senior centers and their participants can do for others who are younger, poorer, and less healthy than themselves. Indeed, senior centers should form partnerships with other groups not only to push for their own interests, but for the interests of others as well. Senior centers should consider becoming advocates for inter-generational cooperation and understanding.

Finally, though it may be a cliche, senior centers will thrive if they continue to do many of the things that have accounted for their success in the past. Senior centers across the nation have shown a great capacity to provide an attractive and supportive environment for elderly persons with different interests and from different backgrounds. This is a strength that must be built on. Change will surely come to senior centers in the next two decades, and at a more rapid pace than has been experienced in the last two. Researchers, planners, policy makers, and practitioners will hopefully learn more about the issues raised in this book so that the future of senior centers and the elderly they serve will be better than the present.

REFERENCES

Soldo, B., & Agree, E. (1988). America's elderly. *Population Bulletin, 43*, 3, September.

Taietz, P. (1976). Two conceptual models of the senior center. *Journal of Gerontology, 31*, 219–222.

Wood, J. (1985). Federal funding cutbacks hard on increasingly popular senior centers. *Perspective on Aging*, September/October, 14–17.

Wood, J., Fox, P., Estes, C., Lee P., & Mahoney, C. (1985). Public policy, the private nonprofit sector, and the delivery of community based long term care services for the elderly. Unpublished manuscript. San Francisco: University of California.

Bibliography

Auerbach, A. (1976). The elderly in rural and urban areas. In L. H. Ginsberg (ed). *Social work in rural communities*. New York: Council on Social Work Education.

Binner, P. (1986). *DRG's and the administration of mental health services*. Englewood Cliffs: Prentice-Hall.

Binstock, R. (1987). Title III of the Older Americans Act: An Analysis and proposal for the 1987 Reauthorization. *The Gerontologist, 27*, 259–265.

Bley, N., M. Goodman, D. Dye, and Z. Harel. (1972). Characteristics of aged participants in an age-segregated leisure program. *The Gerontologist, 12*, 368–370.

Brown, C. and M. O'Day. (1984). Services to the elderly. In N. Gilbert and H. Specht (eds.) *Handbook of Social Services*. Englewood Cliffs: Prentice-Hall.

Carp, F. (1976). A senior center in public housing for the elderly. *The Gerontologist, 16*, 243–249.

Cohen, M. (1972). The multipurpose senior Center. In Senior centers: A focal point for delivery of services to older people. Washington, D.C.: The National Council on the Aging, Inc.

Coward, R. (1979). Planning community services for the rural elderly: Implications for research. *The Gerontologist, 19*, 175–282.

Cryns, A. (1980). A needs assessment survey among elderly residents of the town of Amherst, New York. Report No. 1: Summary of major data trends. Unpublished manuscript, SUNY-Buffalo.

Daum, M. (1982). Preference for age-homogeneous versus age-heterogeneous social integration. *Journal of Gerontological Social Work, 4*, 41–54.

Daum, M., and R. Dobrof. (1983). Seasonal vulnerability to the old and cold: The role of the senior citizen center. *Journal of Gerontological Social Work, 2*, 87–93.

Demko, D. (1980). Utilization, attrition and the senior center. *Journal of Gerontological Social Work, 2*, 87–93.

Downing, J. (1957). Factors affecting the selective use of a social club for the aged. *Journal of Gerontology, 12*, 81–89.

Downing, R., and E. Copeland. (1980). Services for the black elderly. National or local problem? *Journal of Gerontological Social Work, 2*, 289–303.

Estes, C. (1980). *The aging enterprise.* San Francisco: Jossey-Bass Publishers.

Federal Council on Aging. (1978). Public policy and the frail elderly. Washington, D.C.: United States Department of Health, Education and Welfare.

Ferraro, K., and C. Cobb, (1988). Participation in multipurpose senior centers. *Journal of Applied Gerontology, 6*, 429–447.

Fowler, T. (1974). Alternative to the single site center. Washington, D.C.: The National Council on the Aging, Inc.

Frankel, G. (1966). The multipurpose senior citizens center: A new comprehensive agency. *The Gerontologist, 6*, 23–27.

Freedman, R., and M. Axlerod (1952). Who belongs to what in a metropolis. *Adult Leadership, 1*, 6–9.

Gelfand, D. (1984). *The aging network: Programs and services.* New York: Springer Publishing Company.

Gelfand, D., and J. Gelfand (1982). Senior centers and support networks. In D. Seigal and A. Naparstek (eds.) *Community support systems and mental health.* New York: Springer Publishing Company.

Granovetter, M. (1973). The strength of weak ties. *American Journal of Sociology, 78*, 1360–1380.

Guttmann, D., and P. Miller, (1972). Perspectives on the provision of social services in senior centers. *The Gerontologist, 12*, 403–406.

Hanssen, A. M., N. J. Buckspan, L. M. Henderson, B. E. Helbig, and S. H. Zarit (1978). Correlates of senior center participation. *The Gerontologist, 18*, 193–199.

Harris, L. & Associates, Inc. (1975). *The myth and reality of aging in America.* Washington, D.C.: The National Council on the Aging, Inc.

Hirsch, C. (1977). Integrating the nursing home resident into a senior citizens center. *The Gerontologist, 17*, 227–234.

Hoppa, M., and G. Roberts (1974). Implications of the activity factor. *The Gerontologist, 14*, 331–335.

Huttman, E. (1985). *Social services for the elderly.* New York: The Free Press.

Jacobs, B. (1980). Senior centers and the at-risk older person. Washington, D.C.: The National Council on the Aging, Inc.

———. (1982). Educational goals for senior centers: A study of perceptions of reality and aspirations. *Dissertation Abstracts International, 42*, 4253-A.

Jones, E. (1976). An analysis of adult education programs in selected senior citizen centers in Rhode Island. *Dissertation Abstracts International, 37*, 5529-A.

Jordan, J. (1978). Senior center design. An architect's discussion of facility planning. Washington, D.C.: The National Council on the Aging, Inc.

Kendon, J., S. Hughes, P. Campione, and R. Goldberg (1988). Shedding new light on adult day care. *Perspectives on Aging*, November/December, 18–21.

Kent, D. (1978). The how and why of senior centers. *Aging*, May/June, 2–6.

Kim, P. (1981). The low income elderly: Under served victims of public inequity. In P. Kim. and C. Wilson (eds.) *Toward mental health of the rural elderly*, Washington, D.C.: University Press of America.

Krout, J. (1981). Service utilization patterns of the rural elderly. Final report to the Administration on Aging. Fredonia, New York.

————. (1982). Determinants of service use by the aged. Final report to the AARP Andrus Foundation. Fredonia, New York.

————. (1983). Knowledge and use of services by the elderly: A critical review of the literature. *International Journal of Aging and Human Development, 17*, 9–23.

————. (1983). Correlates of senior center utilization. *Research on Aging, 5*, 3, 339–352.

————. (1983). The organization, operation, and programming of senior centers: A national survey. Final report to the AARP Andrus Foundation. Fredonia, New York.

————. (1984). The utilization of formal and informal support by the aged: Rural versus urban differences. Final report to the AARP Andrus Foundation. Fredonia, New York.

————. (1984). Knowledge of senior center activities among the elderly. *Journal of Applied Gerontology, 3*, 71–81.

————. (1984). The organizational characteristics of senior centers in America. *Journal of Applied Gerontology, 3*, 192–205.

————. (1985). Senior center activities and services: Findings from a national survey. *Research on Aging, 7*, 455–471.

————. (1985). Service awareness among the elderly. *Journal of Gerontological Social Work, 9*, 7–18.

————. (1986). Senior center linkages in the community. *The Gerontologist, 26*, 510–515.

————. (1986). *The aged in rural America*. Westport, Connecticut: Greenwood Press.

————. (1987). Senior center linkages and the provision of services to the elderly. Final report to the AARP Andrus Foundation. Fredonia, New York.

————. (1987). Rural versus urban differences in senior center activities and services. *The Gerontologist, 27*, 92–97.

————. (1988). Senior center linkages with community organizations. *Research on Aging, 10*, 258–274.

————. (1988). The frequency, duration, stability, and discontinuation of senior center participation: Causes and consequences. Final report to the AARP Andrus Foundation. Fredonia, New York.

————. (1989). Area agencies on aging: Service planning and provision for the rural elderly. Final report to the Retirement Research Foundation. Fredonia, New York.

————. (1989). The nature and correlates of senior center linkages. *Journal of Applied Gerontology, 8*, 307–322.

Krout, J., S. Cutler, and R. Coward (1989). Correlates of senior center participation: A national analysis. Unpublished manuscript.

Kutner, B., D. Fanshel, A. Togo, and T. Langner (1956). *Five hundred over sixty*. New York: Russell Sage.

Leanse, J. (1977). The senior center, individuals and the community. In R. Kadish (ed.) *The later years: Social applications of gerontology*. Belmont, CA.: Brooks/Cole.

————. (1978). A blend of multi-dimensional activities. *Perspective on Aging, 7*, March/April, 8–13.

Leanse, J., and L. Wagener (1975). Senior centers: A report of senior group programs in America. Washington, D.C.: The National Council on the Aging, Inc.

Lowy, L. (1985). Multipurpose senior centers. In A. Monk (ed.) *Handbook of gerontological services*. New York: Von Nostrand Reinhold Company.

Maryland Association of Senior Centers (1984). Report on MASC survey of senior centers. Unpublished report.

Matthews, S. (1979). *The social world of old women: Management of self-identity.* Newbury Park, CA.: Sage.

Maxwell, J. (1962). Centers for older people: Guide for programs and facilities. Washington, D.C.: The National Council on the Aging, Inc.

May, A., S. Herrman and J. Fitzgerald (1976). An evaluation of congregate meals programs and health of elders. Scott County and Fort Smith Arkansas, Bulletin No. 808, Fayetteville, Arkansas, University of Arkansas.

Meredith, G., and C. Aimor (1976). Indexing the polarization of social groups in a multipurpose senior center. *Psychological Reports, 39,* 88–90.

Moen, E. (1978). The reluctance of the elderly to accept help. *Social Problems, 25,* 293–303.

Monk, A. (1988). The integration of frail elderly into senior centers. Final report to the AARP Andrus Foundation, Columbia University, New York.

Muzzy, C. (1982). Senior centers: Linking the impaired to the community. *Perspective on Aging,* July/August, 22–23.

National Association of State Units on Aging (1983). A profile of state and area agencies on aging (1981). Washington, D.C.

National Center for Health Statistics. Stone, R. (1986). Aging in the eighties, age 65 years and over—Use of community services; Preliminary data from the Supplement on Aging to the National Health Interview Survey: United States, January-June 1984. *Advance Data From Vital and Health Statistics.* No. 124, DHHS, Pub. No. (PHS) 86–1250, September 30, Hyattsville, Maryland: Public Health Service.

National Institute of Senior Centers (1978). *Senior center standards, guidelines for practice.* Washington, D.C.: The National Council for the Aging, Inc.

Oriol, W. (1983). New directions or old themes revisited? The present federal role in service entitlements. *The Gerontologist, 23,* 399–401.

Osgood, M. (1977). Rural and urban attitudes toward welfare. *Social Work, 22,* 41–47.

Poll, S. (1975). The challenge of older adult's satisfaction with participation in a community center. Senior centers: Realizing our potential. Proceedings of the Eighth National Conference of Senior Centers, September, 1973, Chicago, Illinois.

Pothier, W. (1985). Senior centers: An update before it's too late. Unpublished manuscript.

Powers, E. and G. Bultena (1974). Correspondence between anticipated and actual use of public services by the aged. *Social Services Review, 48,* 245–254.

Ralston, P. (1981). Educational needs and activities of older adults: Their relationship to senior center programs. *Educational Gerontology, 7,* 231–244.

———. (1982). Perception of senior centers by the black elderly: A comparative study. *Journal of Gerontological Social Work, 4,* 127–137.

———. (1983). Senior centers in rural communities: A qualitative study. Paper presented at the Annual Meeting of the Gerontological Society of America, San Francisco.

———. (1983). Levels of senior centers: A broadened view of group based programs for the elderly. *Activities, Adaptation, and Aging, 3,* 79–91.

———. (1984). Senior center utilization by black elderly adults: Social, attitudinal and knowledge correlates. *Journal of Gerontology, 39,* 224–229.

———. (1984). Senior center research: Concept, programs and utilization. Paper presented at the Annual Meeting of the Gerontological Society of America, San Antonio, Texas.

————. (1985). Determinants of senior center attendance. Paper presented at the Annual Meeting of the Gerontological Society of America, New Orleans.

————. (1985). Senior center utilization by black elderly adults: Social, attitudinal and knowledge correlates. *Journal of Gerontology, 39*, 224–229.

————. (1987). Senior center research: Policy from knowledge? In E. Borgatta and R. Montgomery (eds.) *Critical issues in aging policy: Linking research and values.* Newbury Park, Ca.: Sage.

Ralston, P., and M. Griggs. (1985). Factors affecting utilization of senior centers: Race, sex and socioeconomic differences. *Journal of Gerontological Social Work, 9*, 99–111.

Ries, I. (1982). Hearing ability of persons by sociodemographic and health characteristics: United States: National Center for Health Statistics. *Vital Health Studies*, Series 10, No. 140, DHHS Pub No. (PNS) 82–1568, Public Health Services, Washington, D.C.: United States Government Printing Office.

Rosen, C., R. J. Vandenberg, and S. Rosen, (1981). The fate of senior center dropouts. In P. Kim & C. Wilson (eds.) *Toward mental health of the rural elderly.* Washington, D.C.: University Press of America, Inc.

Rosenzweig, N. (1975). Some difference between elderly people who use community resources and those who do not. *Journal of the American Geriatrics Society, XXIII*, 224–233.

Rosow, I. (1967). *Social integration of the aged.* New York: Free Press.

Schneider, M., D. Chapman, and D. Voth (1985). Senior center participation: A two-stage approach to impact evaluation. *The Gerontologist, 25*, 194–200.

Schramm, W., and R. Storey (1962). *Little House: A study of senior centers.* Stanford: Institute for Communication Research.

Schulder, D. (1985). Older Americans Act: A vast network of public, private agencies. *Perspective on Aging, 14*, 5–7.

Scott, J. (1983). Older rural adults: Perspectives on status and needs. Paper presented at the annual meeting of American Home Economics Association, Milwaukee.

Sela, I. (1986). A study of programs and services for the hearing impaired elderly in senior centers and clubs in the U.S. Unpublished dissertation. Washington, D.C.: Galludet College.

Short, P., and J. Leon (1988). National estimates of the use of formal home and community services by the functionally impaired elderly. Paper presented at the annual conference of the Gerontological Society of America, San Francisco.

Silverstein, N. (1984). Informing the elderly about public services: The relationship between sources of knowledge and service utilization. *The Gerontologist, 24*, 37–40.

Silvey, R. (1962). Participation in a senior citizens day center. In J. Kaplan and G. J. Aldridge (eds.) *Social welfare of the aging.* New York: Columbia University Press.

Snider, E. (1980). Factors influencing health service knowledge among the elderly. *Journal of Health and Social Behavior, 21*, 371–377.

————. (1980). Awareness and use of health services by the elderly: A Canadian study. *Medical Care, 18*, 1177–1182.

Soldo, B. (1980). America's elderly in the 1980's. *Population Bulletin, 35*.

Soldo, B., and E. Agree. (1988). America's elderly. *Population Bulletin, 43*, 3, September.

Storey, R. (1962). Who attends a senior activity center? A comparison of Little House members with non-members in the same community. *The Gerontologist, 2*, 216–222.

Taietz, P. (1970). *Community structure and aging*. Ithaca, New York: Cornell University.

———. (1976). Two conceptual models of the senior center. *Journal of Gerontology, 31*, 219–222.

Tissue, T. (1971). Social class and the senior citizen center. *The Gerontologist, 11*, 196–200.

Toseland, R., and J. Sykes (1977). Senior citizens center participation and other correlates of life satisfaction. *The Gerontologist, 17*, 235–241.

Trela, J. (1976). Social class and association membership: An analysis of age-graded and non-age graded voluntary participation. *Journal of Gerontology, 31*, 198–203.

Trela, J., and L. Simmons (1971). Health and other factors affecting membership and attrition in a senior center. *Journal of Gerontology, 26*, 46–51.

Tuckman, J. (1967). Factors related to attendance in a center for older people. *Journal of American Geriatrics Society, 15*, 474–479.

United States Department of Health and Human Services. (1987) Older Americans Act of 1965, As Amended. Washington, D.C.: U.S.G.P.O.

United States Department of Health and Human Services. (1988). Final regulations, Older American Act: Grants for State and Community Programs on Aging. Washington, D.C.: U.S.G.P.O.

United States Government Printing Office (1981). 1981 White House Conference on Aging: Report of the mini-conference on senior centers. Washington, D.C.

United States Senate (1979). Older Americans Act: A staff summary. Washington, D.C.: United States Government Printing Office.

Wagener, L. (1981). The senior center: A partner in the community care system. Washington, D.C.: The National Council on the Aging, Inc.

———. (1981). The concept of a focal point for service delivery in the field of aging. Washington, D.C.: The National Council on the Aging, Inc.

Wagener, L., and P. Carter (1982). Building community partnerships. Washington, D.C.: The National Council on the Aging, Inc.

Ward, R., S. Sherman, and M. LaGory (1984). Informal networks and knowledge of services for older persons. *Journal of Gerontology, 31*, 216–223.

Weber, M. (1947). *The theory of social and economic organization*. New York: Free Press.

Weiss, T. (1986). A legislative view of Medicare and DRG's. *American Psychologist, 41*, 79–82.

White House Conference on the Aging. (1982). Final report: The 1981 White House Conference on the Aging. 3 Vols. Washington, D.C.: The Conference.

Woolf, L. (1982). How senior centers grew through three WHCoAs. *Perspective on Aging, 11*, 13–17.

Index

ABOUT THE AUTHOR

JOHN A. KROUT received his Ph.D. in Sociology from Penn State University in 1977 and is a Professor of Sociology at the State University of New York College at Fredonia. Dr. Krout has been an active scholar and teacher in the field of aging since 1980. He has published over twenty articles in a wide range of academic journals including *The Gerontologist*, *Research on Aging*, *Journal of Applied Gerontology*, and *The International Journal of Aging and Human Development*. He has presented thirty papers at national, regional and state conferences. His research on senior centers has been supported by the Administration on Aging and by several grants from the AARP Andrus Foundation. He has published two books for Greenwood Press, both on rural aging. Dr. Krout belongs to ten professional organizations and was recently named a fellow of the Gerontological Society of America. He is a member of the executive board of the New York State Association of Gerontological Educators and also serves as secretary of the Delegate Council of the National Center on Rural Aging—a unit of the National Council of the Aging.